PENGUIN BOOKS

ACCEPTANCE

David L. Marcus is the author of *What It Takes to Pull Me Through*, a look at the secret lives of teenagers. He has been an education writer and foreign correspondent at *U.S. News & World Report*, the *Boston Globe*, the *Miami Herald*, and the *Dallas Morning News*, where he was the cowinner of a Pulitzer Prize. After a stint as a high school teacher, he returned to journalism as a writer for *Newsday*. A graduate of Brown University, Marcus was a Nieman Fellow at Harvard. He frequently speaks to schools, churches, and community groups about adolescence, education, and college admissions. Visit his Web site at www.DaveMarcus.com.

TO JUSTINE,

who inspires me, guides me, and keeps me laughing

AND TO BENJIE, TATIANA, ALEXA, AND DASHIELL,

who make the journey complete

To Emily

Enjoy!

Acceptance

A LEGENDARY GUIDANCE COUNSELOR

HELPS SEVEN KIDS FIND THE RIGHT COLLEGES—

AND FIND THEMSELVES

David L. Marcus

PENGUIN BOOKS

PENGUIN BOOKS
Published by the Penguin Group
Penguin Group (USA) Inc., 375 Hudson Street, New York, New York 10014, U.S.A.
Penguin Group (Canada), 90 Eglinton Avenue East, Suite 700, Toronto,
Ontario, Canada M4P 2Y3 (a division of Pearson Penguin Canada Inc.)
Penguin Books Ltd, 80 Strand, London WC2R 0RL, England
Penguin Ireland, 25 St Stephen's Green, Dublin 2, Ireland (a division of Penguin Books Ltd)
Penguin Group (Australia), 250 Camberwell Road, Camberwell,
Victoria 3124, Australia (a division of Pearson Australia Group Pty Ltd)
Penguin Books India Pvt Ltd, 11 Community Centre, Panchsheel Park, New Delhi – 110 017, India
Penguin Group (NZ), 67 Apollo Drive, Rosedale, North Shore 0632,
New Zealand (a division of Pearson New Zealand Ltd)
Penguin Books (South Africa) (Pty) Ltd, 24 Sturdee Avenue,
Rosebank, Johannesburg 2196, South Africa

Penguin Books Ltd, Registered Offices:
80 Strand, London WC2R 0RL, England

First published in the United States of America by The Penguin Press,
a member of Penguin Group (USA) Inc. 2009
Published in Penguin Books 2010

1 3 5 7 9 10 8 6 4 2

THE LIBRARY OF CONGRESS HAS CATALOGED THE HARDCOVER EDITION AS FOLLOWS:
Marcus, Dave (David L.)
Acceptance : a legendary guidance counselor helps seven kids find
the right colleges—and find themselves / David L. Marcus.
p. cm.
ISBN 978-1-59420-214-8 (hc.)
ISBN 978-0-14-311764-3 (pbk.)
1. College choice—United States.   2. Educational counseling—New York (State)—
North Shore (Long Island)   3. Smith, Gwyeth.   4. Student counselors—
New York (State)—North Shore (Long Island)—Biography.   I. Title.
LB2350.5.M34 2009
378.1'610973—dc22   2009008328

Printed in the United States of America
DESIGNED BY AMANDA DEWEY

CONTENTS

One More Year

I n a small office at the back of a deserted high school, Gwyeth Smith Jr. was puzzling over the college admissions season that had recently ended—the cruelest in his thirty-plus years of working with applicants.

Smitty, as friends called him, was the director of guidance at Oyster Bay High School on Long Island's North Shore. He had close-cropped salt-and-pepper hair, a matching mustache and beard, and looked younger than his sixty-two years. It was a humid morning in August 2007, a week before the start of classes, and he was clearing his desk to prepare for the fall rush. He studied a newspaper clipping about a nearby school's dismal luck with the Ivy League.

PRINCETON: 4 of 5 rejected
YALE: 5 of 6 rejected
BROWN: 11 of 12 rejected
HARVARD: 7 of 8 rejected, and 1 wait-listed

The school, Northport High, prided itself on its two dozen Advanced Placement courses, its arts program, and its service project in Central America. Little of that had swayed the Ivies this time. In all, Harvard, Yale, Princeton, and Brown had accepted just three of Northport's thirty-one applications.

Every high school in the area except Oyster Bay had been hit hard by rejections. A few miles away, the Mineola guidance department was baffled by MIT's snub of their salutatorian, a science whiz with near-perfect SATs. At John F. Kennedy High, on the South Shore, eight of nine University of Pennsylvania applicants were turned down, along with all seven who tried for Washington University in St. Louis. Across the country, counselors could list student council presidents, Eagle Scouts and scholar-athletes who'd been spurned by first-, second-, and third-choice schools.

The acceptance rates at the colleges explained why. Penn took only 15.9 percent of applicants, Stanford 10.3 percent, Columbia 8.9 percent. Duke rebuffed more than half of the 1,381 valedictorians who applied. And it wasn't just the elite private schools. Binghamton, of the State University of New York system, had gotten so many early applications that thousands had to be put off for decision until spring. Even safety schools were no longer safe: The University of Miami, once derided as "Suntan U," got nearly twenty thousand applications for two thousand openings.

And yet Smitty was serene. Most of the kids at his small public high school were admitted to their first-choice colleges, and many had sorted through competing offers. A boy who floundered at the start of the admissions process was accepted at all seven schools he applied to; he'd chosen Rice over Cornell. One girl hadn't just gotten into MIT, she had actually *rejected* MIT. Instead, she accepted a scholarship to Case Western Reserve, where professors requested her help on a research project.

Smitty had made sure that Oyster Bay was one of the first districts in the area to buy software called Naviance, which displayed scattergrams with students' scores and GPAs and a summary of where they'd been accepted or rejected. With a couple of clicks, Smitty was reminded that Penn had admitted one girl even though twenty-three kids in the senior class had had better grades. A few more clicks showed where other Oyster Bay students were heading. Duke, Cornell, University of Chicago, Brown, NYU, Northwestern, George Washington University, Rice, Tufts, Boston University, Barnard, Berklee College of Music, McGill, Michigan, Wisconsin, Delaware . . .

What made the acceptances more remarkable was that Oyster Bay was not a school of national stature. For decades it had been overshadowed by its neighbors, Syosset, Cold Spring Harbor, and Jericho, which dominated science competitions and churned out National Merit finalists. Some of the best public schools in the country could be found across the Long Island Sound: Scarsdale and Chappaqua, Greenwich and Westport. And just down the road were the academic bastions of Great Neck and Port Washington, better known to generations of *The Great Gatsby* readers as West Egg and East Egg.

But Oyster Bay had Smitty. Parents called him the "guidance guru." Few counselors, they said, lived and breathed the applications game like Smitty. He could find the perfect school for the most quirky kid, coax a sensitive essay from the toughest jock, and induce the nerdiest engineering student to exude poise in an interview.

Legend had it that Smitty was so well connected he could simply pick up the phone and request that a college make space. That, of course, was an exaggeration, but Smitty was so gifted at getting the absolute best out of his kids that he got them to open doors that otherwise might have been closed. At every step, he pestered them, championed them, and encouraged them. He nudged students into difficult courses, drilled them before they took the SATs, and relentlessly made them revise their essays.

"The application process is all about discovering who you are." That was one of Smitty's sayings. So was, "Everyone has a story to tell." His job, he liked to say, was not to simply flaunt scores but to get students to present their most compelling selves to admissions offices.

Smitty's mystique helped him get away with telling parents some blunt truths. As a father went on about how his daughter *had* to get into Emory's premed program, Smitty's cheeks would redden. "Sir, with all respect," he'd interject in his gravelly voice, "are we talking about your ambition or hers?"

Smitty had become known beyond Oyster Bay. A few years earlier, *Worth* named the fifty public schools with the highest percentage of graduates going to Harvard, Yale, and Princeton. Four Long Island powerhouses made the list, and so did the little upstart Oyster Bay. Although Smitty enjoyed the resulting accolades, he believed the magazine's premise was superficial. He worried about the increasing emphasis on a handful of prestigious universities. While he encouraged applicants to aim high, he also pushed kids to look beyond brand names for the right fit. He tried to get his "youngstahs," as he called them in his native Maine accent, to see where they were headed long-term—to view college not as an admissions prize but as a path to becoming a pediatrician, teacher, YouTube engineer, you name it.

When he looked back at the past season, his proudest achievements were not Ivy acceptances but the months he spent helping students reveal their best truths. He thought of the boy who came to terms with his father's death while writing his applications, or the girl, a first-generation American, who wrote revealingly about her dad growing up in Paraguay with one pair of shoes.

As Smitty sorted through his papers, a slender, six-foot-tall boy with short brown hair cleared his throat at the doorway. Every year, Smitty took on several students as special projects. Jeff Sanders was one.

Although he was among the most popular kids in school, some teachers saw him as a slacker.

But Smitty appreciated things in Jeff that those teachers missed. He was a three-sport athlete who wanted to go into sports management. Even now, he scouted community and high school players to help them get recruited, writing reports for a Web site read by coaches.

Jeff was a selfless kid in more ways than that. Smitty had heard, for example, that the boy's family had taken in several relatives who were in crisis, something Jeff never talked about. He often stayed home on weekends to look after his young cousins while other students partied.

Jeff was also an enthusiastic kid, perhaps too much so. He was ready to rush his college hunt despite a problem—he still hadn't stepped up as a student. Smitty knew that was now essential. Jeff would have to deliver better grades, and find a compelling way to tell his story in his applications.

Jeff sat down in Smitty's office, and after small talk about their summer vacations, they focused on Jeff's college hopes. He reported that he'd already chosen a school where he wanted to apply early. He'd have to finish the package in seven weeks, which worried Smitty. He knew that meant the most current grades the admissions office would see would come from Jeff's junior year.

Smitty turned the conversation to Jeff's record. If he remembered correctly, the boy's grade point average was 78.1. He pulled up Jeff's stats on the computer to check, and he was right: 78.1. Smitty swiveled around in his black executive chair and looked Jeff in the eye. He felt his job at such a time was to be honest, not blindly supportive.

"Before we get into early applications or any applications at all, you need to demonstrate you can handle the kind of work you'll get in college." His pitch lowered. "I'm not sure what went wrong, young man, but you had a dismal junior year. When an admissions committee sees that GPA, you'll get blown out of the water."

He told Jeff that early decision would be a bad idea. He needed to pump up his transcript first—not just in grades but in the quality of his classes. Smitty knew admissions staffs look at both factors. He suggested that Jeff switch out of Discrete Math, which taught the basics for consumers, and take precalculus instead. He also suggested that Jeff take physics. If he did well with such challenges, it would show colleges he was academically serious. Smitty knew that was asking a lot of Jeff, but he'd learned that if you push kids, they'll step up.

"You're going to be very busy," Smitty said.

"I've been busy my whole life. I like being busy. I go crazy if I'm sitting around doing nothing."

Smitty wanted to make sure the boy left on a positive note. "You're smart, you're a leader, you've got so much going for you," he said. "You need to throw yourself into academics as energetically as you throw yourself into everything else. I have no doubt you can do it."

"Don't worry, Mr. Smith," Jeff assured him.

Smitty was also hoping that Jeff would be motivated by his girlfriend. Jenna took difficult courses, turned in assignments early, and had a 107.7 GPA, making her the salutatorian. She wanted to apply to Harvard, Columbia, and Brown. If some of her work ethic rubbed off, Smitty felt, Jeff would have a shot at a selective college. If it didn't, he wouldn't.

Smitty had decided that this would be his last year on the job. His colleagues at high schools across the country were bracing for another difficult application season, with a record 3.3 million students in America's class of 2008. Fear of this competition would drive kids to send out more applications, which would only make things worse. This final year, Smitty knew, would be unlike any he'd had since starting his career in 1971.

While Jeff Sanders was one of Smitty's special projects, he had thirty other kids to personally worry about. Every spring, Smitty handpicked advisees from the junior class. He liked a cross section: a handful of hard-luck cases, a few unfocused kids, some who were middle of-the-road, and several top performers aiming for big-name universities.

Five of his advisees particularly intrigued him. There was Jeff, who now knew he needed to step up his game quickly. Allyson, an excellent student, fretted that admissions officers would dismiss her as just another Jewish overachiever from the suburbs. Chelsea was gifted at writing and photography, but procrastinated badly. Lee felt pressure to live up to the Ivy expectations in his Korean American community. And Riana, an African American girl, had lived with expectations that weren't high enough.

As he sat in his office on this hot August day, Smitty was already plotting the college quest for these five and the dozens of others from Oyster Bay who faced what would likely prove the toughest admissions year ever.

Yale Loves Me;
Yale Loves Me Not

Soon after moving to the suburbs of New York a few years ago, I wrote a series of newspaper stories about students applying to college. I met private consultants who steer kids into advanced classes and exotic internships to impress admissions staffs. I wrote about parents going to a college fair . . . at an elementary school.

In the prosperous village of Jericho, I asked a mother when the college-admissions frenzy starts. "In utero," she said.

Since my days as a high school senior, a new industry had been born. It was built around getting affluent kids into the fifty or so most prestigious colleges. One Manhattan consultant started working with students as early as ninth grade, and charged forty thousand dollars—as much as a year at some private colleges. The rich had become engaged in an admissions arms race. That left middle- and lower-class families at a disadvantage. They couldn't afford packagers. All they had were how-to books and Web sites—and, if they were very lucky, an exceptional guidance counselor.

Far more than people realize, a wise college counselor can make the difference in getting in. Perhaps more important, the best counselors understand their job isn't just knowing the world of financial aid, or the difference between the filmmaking programs at NYU and USC; it's helping teenagers see their strengths, their potential, and how to make those things come alive in an application to the right school.

As part of my newspaper series, I set out to find one such counselor. When I asked Long Island parents and principals, the same answer kept coming back: "See Smitty." They meant Gwyeth (rhymes with *faith*) Smith Jr. of Oyster Bay High. One mother told me she bought a house in the district because of his reputation.

And so, one morning at the start of admissions season, I drove to Oyster Bay High, a stately eighty-year-old brick building just up the hill from the Long Island Sound. Smitty was waiting for me in the guidance office, and for the next hour, in his reassuring Maine accent, he told anecdotes of bright kids who choke on the SATs, of parents who meddle too much, of the essay that saved an applicant's candidacy, and of his life's goal of helping students onto the best path after high school.

To watch Smitty in action, I flew to Pittsburgh for an admissions conference that attracted five thousand participants. While other counselors ordered morning coffee, Smitty was roving the campus of nearby Duquesne University, checking the student union and grilling undergrads about their classes. Later, at the convention center overlooking the Allegheny River, he greeted admissions deans, asking by name about their spouses, their children, and, at one point, even a dog.

D on't apply to Harvard."
It was the only time my father offered advice on my college hunt. My dad had gone to Bard in the early 1940s. It was a freewheeling campus

above the Hudson River. He loved it, but halfway through he went off to World War II, and returned to finish at Harvard. After Bard, he told me, Harvard struck him as too impersonal for undergrads.

My guidance counselor's main role was making sure I had enough credits to graduate. For my college tour, I boarded an Amtrak up the New England coast. My first stop was New Haven, where I strolled through Gothic archways, eavesdropped on dining hall conversations, and fell under Yale's spell.

Two of my brightest classmates, David and Teddy, also applied. I knew Yale wouldn't accept three kids from Hartsdale, New York. Realizing I needed to outshine them somehow, I wrote an essay on how I was smitten by everything Yale, from the small seminars to the deep-blue T-shirts. I sent it to the *New York Times,* which published it on the cover of its education section under the headline YALE LOVES ME; YALE LOVES ME NOT. The *Times* included a drawing of a gawky teenager—a fair depiction of me—gazing into a mirror at the image of a broad-shouldered young man smoking a pipe and wearing a sweater with a big Y.

Yale rejected me anyway, and accepted my two classmates.

I ended up at Brown, in Providence. I disliked college for the first year, then connected with an inspiring history professor, began exploring the city's old world richness, and gradually felt I was where I belonged. I got over my pangs for Yale.

I later learned that one of my classmates dropped out of Yale. Not long ago, I e-mailed the other to ask how he liked it. His answer reflected what I have come to see as the core philosophy of Gwyeth Smith Jr. of Oyster Bay High.

"If you're there for the right reasons," he wrote back, "you'll love it. But going because you feel you should go or because people will be impressed are not the right reasons."

His e-mail echoed lessons I'd learned as a higher-education reporter for

U.S. News & World Report. My assignments took me to many little-known colleges that had transformed students, from Alma College in Michigan to Simpson in Iowa. I realized there are hundreds of great schools out there.

At one point, I came across the same realization in my own life. After I graduated Brown, with a goal of working as a foreign correspondent, I took a nighttime Spanish class at a community college in West Palm Beach. My Spanish courses at Brown had been taught by grad students more interested in discussing Cervantes than teaching the language. The community college took a more pragmatic approach. That's where I learned to speak Spanish, and eventually, thanks to my time at a campus with all the appeal of a strip mall, I became a foreign correspondent.

As I spent months watching Smitty advise students, I realized he was applying the same lessons my father had passed along. It's not about the brand; it's about the fit. In Smitty's eyes, this had to do with seventeen year olds thinking through a first big step toward adulthood. He realized that American teens have few rites of passage. Applying to colleges was one of those milestones. Though he wasn't the kind to speak of it in these terms, he viewed himself as an elder helping them through this ritual.

Smitty had other principles you don't hear in every counselor's office. He felt the application process wasn't just about getting in, but about awakening kids to themselves, and to a life's path. He tried to make students see college not as an end, but a start.

When he felt a student wasn't ready for higher education, he urged parents to consider a "gap year" of work, travels, or public service. He usually lost that argument. Mothers and fathers usually felt their kids needed to keep up with their peers. Only later, when their children struggled at college, would many parents see he was right.

When Smitty announced his plans to retire, I decided to chronicle his last year. I'd read many books about the college pursuit, but never one focused on the crucial role of an exceptional guidance counselor.

I was especially intrigued by Oyster Bay High, a public school with kids from all backgrounds. I wanted to see how Smitty and these students competed with privileged kids who had the dual advantages of a prep school background and private admissions consultants. One such consultant, Elizabeth Wissner-Gross, had a busy practice near Oyster Bay. In her guide, *What Colleges Don't Tell You,* she warned, "Summer is your child's chance to win the edge, to beat the competition. . . . By fall, your son or daughter should possess an entirely new repertoire of abilities. Don't let your children waste their summers 'hanging out.'"

Smitty took a different approach. He told parents that teenagers—even high school seniors—need to be children at times, and not get swallowed by the application frenzy. He felt kids' best chance of getting in was not to package themselves but to reveal themselves.

This seemed the perfect time to observe an admissions wizard at work. When I watched Smitty in 2007–2008, parts of the game were changing. Harvard, Princeton, and the University of Virginia had just abandoned early decision programs. Economic turbulence made families everywhere take a closer look at state universities. Most intriguing to me was Smitty himself. I didn't want to write a book about status-obsessed applicants from exclusive high schools getting into Harvard; I wanted to show how a special counselor applied nearly four decades of knowledge to help Main Street students find, and afford, the right school.

In short, I wanted to see not how to "win" the admissions game, but how one man teaches students to play it in the way that charts the best course for their lives.

Cast of Characters

THE ADULTS

Gwyeth Smith Jr., guidance director

Kathi Reilly, English teacher

Matt Brown, social worker

THE SEVEN STUDENTS

Jeff Sanders, a jock struggling to become a more focused student despite upheaval at home

Allyson Frankel, who worries admissions offices will see her as just another Jewish girl from the suburbs with good scores

Chelsea Flynn, a free spirit who loves writing and photography

Lee Kim, a conflicted overachiever who wants to honor his Korean immigrant parents but find his own way

Riana Tyson, a black student stressed by an overloaded schedule as she seeks the college diploma her parents never got

Nathaniel Coleman, whose mother is involved in choosing the college where he will study engineering

Layla Eran, the valedictorian who often stays at school late into the night

OTHER STUDENTS

Jenna, the salutatorian who wants to go to college near home

Colin, a crew star being recruited by Ivy schools

Curtis, still having surgery from a childhood disease and searching for a scholarship after his father abandoned the family

Dominique, an actress applying to theater programs

Kasper, an Iranian American whose dad was killed by a train just before the start of senior year

Andreas, a loner with hidden struggles from his brother's death

ONE

The First Day of the Rest of Your Life

Name: Jeff Sanders

Weighted GPA: 78.1—85th in the class of 109

SAT: 550 critical reading + 600 math = 1150 composite

ACT: not taken

On the first period of the first day of his last year of high school, Jeff Sanders bounded up three steps at a time. It was 7:52 A.M., and he was two minutes late for his English elective, Essay Writing for College. Inside room 207, the pile of paperbacks atop a library cart included *The College Board Book of Majors,* and on a nearby shelf, the *College Handbook* reviewed almost four thousand two- and four-year schools.

The essay class was taught by Jeff's college counselor, Gwyeth Smith Jr., and a popular teacher, Ms. Kathi Reilly. Mr. Smith wore a white shirt, blue tie, and navy jacket—he dressed up for school, just as he did on fall afternoons when he worked as the scorekeeper at Jeff's football games.

The seventeen seniors in the class settled into chairs around a long conference table.

"Welcome to the first day of the rest of your life," Mr. Smith announced.

"It will be a roller coaster," Ms. Reilly added. She was talking about the application process ahead. "You'll have a lot of highs and lows."

"And you'll have fun," Mr. Smith assured them.

Jeff wasn't so sure about that.

Mr. Smith explained that the course was meant not just to help kids with their essays but also with time management. He'd seen too many youngsters turn in bad applications because they waited until the last minute.

They'd started the course seven years ago to give kids one period a day to consider colleges and write their essays. At first it was a single class that attracted a few curious students; now it was Oyster Bay's most popular elective, offered by two teachers and several counselors five periods a day to 70 of the school's 109 seniors. Smith felt the interest reflected the times as well as the course itself. The college race had become more obsessive than ever.

A couple of air conditioners wheezed from the room's tall windows, but it was still hot and stuffy. Ms. Reilly asked the kids why they'd decided to take this class when they could have opted for a free first period, and extra sleep.

"I need some guidance," Jeff said simply.

"I don't know if I have the diligence to do it on my own," admitted Lee, a Korean American boy who many assumed was headed to an Ivy.

"I want to spend quality time with you," a girl told Ms. Reilly to laughter.

Ms. Reilly posed the next question, "How many of you have parents who are driving you crazy?" She meant about applications.

Most of the kids raised their hands.

"How many of you describe yourselves as procrastinators?"

This time, everybody raised a hand.

Mr. Smith asked if anyone was applying early to a college. A third of the kids said yes, including Jeff. Mr. Smith explained that "early decision" meant a November deadline and a pledge to cancel applications elsewhere if admitted in mid-December. "Early action" had the same schedule, but no pledge. The upside was that early applicants had better odds and a quick verdict. The downside was the November 1 deadline.

By now, the mood in the room had grown somber, so Ms. Reilly asked the kids what they'd done over the summer. Jeff had scooped ice cream, Chelsea had taught kids to sail, and Lee had attended a youth leadership conference that included a trip to visit inmates in Sing Sing prison. A few kids had traveled overseas. Some had been babysitters, camp counselors, and one was a short-order cook.

Mr. Smith liked those answers. He knew too many students who programmed their summers to look good on applications. It was fine to take courses in multivariable calculus, but he also believed in the benefits of busing tables—a bit of normalcy in overpressured young lives.

Ms. Reilly asked the students to describe their admissions hopes and fears. No one mentioned hopes.

"I'm gonna have a nervous breakdown," said Dominique, an aspiring actress.

Others said they'd never make it through the next few months.

"Trust us," Ms. Reilly assured them. "We haven't lost one yet."

Smitty had been a guidance counselor at a half dozen New York area school districts, and had spent the past eight years at Oyster Bay High. It was surrounded by the Gold Coast communities where prosperous New Yorkers once summered. Theodore Roosevelt came to his Sagamore Hill estate as president. "There could be no healthier and pleasanter place in which to bring up children," T.R. said, "than in the nook of old-time America around Sagamore Hill." Billy Joel, media tycoon Rupert Murdoch, and former mob boss John "Junior" Gotti lived in the area. The hamlet of Oyster Bay was less ritzy, having evolved as a service center for the rich. The tight-packed neighborhoods were home to tradespeople, small business owners, and a few baymen who still raked the harbor for clams. Oyster Bay had an Irish population, Italians, Hispanics, a few African Americans, and, in recent years, Muslim immigrants from South Asia.

Unlike the suburban sprawl typical of Long Island, downtown Oyster Bay was a picturesque commercial center. It had a modest hardware store and a hot dog stand as well as a Pilates studio and a fancy restaurant featuring semolina-dusted calamari with caper rémoulade.

Mostly, Oyster Bay was about families. On a typical summer day, children kayaked in the harbor and played on the lawns and beach of Theodore Roosevelt Memorial Park. On weekday evenings, commuters returned home on the train from Manhattan on the west side of downtown. Going east along Main Street, there was a public library, a volunteer firehouse, and an Episcopal church with a plaque marking T.R.'s pew. The most prominent building of all was Oyster Bay High.

The school was built in the self-confident 1920s, a solid four-story redbrick fortress on an embankment. The interior was in the American Hospital style, with several hallways painted pale blue. The eastern half of the building echoed with the sounds of band musicians, while the western half smelled of French fries drifting up the stairs from the cafeteria. In a courtyard, a science teacher kept a rooster, who declared his presence amid the din of allegiance pledging and morning announcements.

As the first day of Essay Writing for College in room 207 was coming to a close, Smitty was regaling his students on the finer points of standardized testing. "There will be some colleges that will say, 'We will take either the SAT or the ACT, plus either two or three SAT IIs.' There will be a greater number that take the SAT and the SAT II or the ACT, so if you just take the ACT you may reduce a piece of the testing. Everybody clear on that?"

The kids stared blankly.

As many of the students knew, Smitty and Kathi, both divorced, lived together. Sometimes, Kathi finished Smitty's sentences—or even stopped them, as she did this time. "Save that for tomorrow!" she said, to chuckles.

The start of every school year brought its surprises, this year a sad one. A few weeks earlier, Smitty had gotten a call about Kasper, the highest-ranked boy in the class. His father, a doctor and Iranian immigrant, had been killed by a train while crossing the tracks in a summer storm. Kasper approached Kathi at the end of the first day of school. Somehow, even while mourning his father, he'd written his essay for the Common Application, used by hundreds of schools.

"It's done," he announced to Kathi. "You can look at it if you want."

"Already?" she asked. She slipped it into her canvas bag. It was the first of the season and she was glad to get it. But she and Smitty took essays seriously—as a key part of an application, and something to refine and refine again.

"I'll be happy to read this," she said, "but I'm warning you, it might not really be done."

Smitty chose not to tell the kids about all they faced. He knew, for example, that some would be accepted into their first choice, then learn they didn't get enough aid to afford it. Most of Oyster Bay High's families were working- and middle-class. Many couldn't take on big loans or pay fifty thousand dollars a year in college costs. Every spring, just before deposits were due at colleges, several families abandoned private school hopes and sent their kids to SUNY, the State University of New York.

Smitty also knew that a few months after these kids at last went to college, he'd get a few panicky e-mails from those convinced they'd made the wrong choice. It's why he always pushed families to make sure of the fit. Switching schools was disruptive and sometimes costly, since colleges rarely awarded transfers as good a financial package as freshmen received.

Smitty realized that money was a big issue this year. He could predict a recession before some economists could. Recently, a father confided he was having trouble making the mortgage. Another canceled his school fund-raiser donations. A family with one son at a private college said the second son would have to go to a state school. These were hard times.

For now, Smitty was focused on a more immediate problem: Jeff Sanders's grades. When they'd discussed colleges in August, Jeff said he liked George Mason University in Virginia, Sacred Heart in Connecticut, and Seton Hall in New Jersey. Most of all, he liked Fordham, and wanted to apply there early.

Smitty was close with Fordham's vice president for enrollment management, but he knew that wouldn't help in this case. Jeff's GPA was 78.1. C-plus. That would not get him in.

Jeff was a jock, but there was a twist that set him apart. As good as he was, as much as he lived for sports, Jeff recognized that getting recruited to play in college is tough, and that many high school stars don't make the cut. He was able to accept that he wouldn't, at last not at the highest level, Division I. His main sport was basketball, and he'd worked his heart out at it, but he knew he didn't have the height or top-tier talent for D-I. Plenty of players are equally thrilled to play at the D-III level, which is highly competitive, but those are mostly smaller schools, like Colorado College, Middlebury, and Denison.

Jeff wanted to major in sports management at a big university, and felt it would help him more to be, say, a manager for a Division I team than a player on D III. Smitty was impressed that Jeff could put his athlete's ego second by supporting others from the sidelines instead of being on the court.

But it posed a problem. Now that Jeff wasn't going to college as an athlete, there would be no coach helping open doors for him at admissions. Jeff would have to rely even more on his grades and board scores. Pushing them higher would take a superhuman effort in the first two quarters of senior year. Some teachers doubted he could do it. He was known for being distracted in class.

Still, Smitty saw a sign of hope. The boy had taken the SATs with no preparation and gotten 1150—which correlated to a B-plus average at many schools. Jeff was a typical underachiever, strong in activities, weak in class. Smitty had a soft spot for such kids, and he wanted to know why Jeff's grades didn't reflect his ability.

As a little boy, Jeff had been known as "the mayor" in his neighborhood because of his ability to win over strangers. In middle school, he began to watch and interview high school basketball players, then write profiles about them for a Web site that tracked athletes. Coaches started to e-mail Jeff with questions about recruits, and a few even called to invite him to dinner, assuming he was a professional sportswriter. His father would take the phone and ask, "Do you know that Jeff is fifteen?" then wait for the silence.

By senior year, Jeff had become a force on campus. He was cocaptain of the varsity football and basketball teams, and he played on the tennis team in the spring. Evenings, Jeff worked at an ice cream parlor. Some nights, he volunteered with the fire department, and he was training to become an emergency medical technician.

At one point, he'd even helped get a kid into college. Jeff played basketball on a community team, facing off against a six-feet-six-inch senior who was a standout rebounder. Jeff learned that the boy's father had died and his mom was addicted to crack. The two became friends, and because of his Web site work, Jeff knew of a Florida community college looking for a player with his skills. Jeff took it upon himself to call the school's coach, and soon the team had a newly recruited rebounder.

Smitty had come to admire Jeff's even temper as much as his big heart. Months before, Jeff's beloved seventeen-year-old Buick LeSabre was stolen while he was playing in a basketball tournament. When the police found it on a highway, it had been stripped clean. Even the steering wheel was gone; the only thing left was a basketball trophy in the trunk. Smitty asked Jeff what he planned to do.

"Same as everyone else, I guess. I'm making money to buy another car."

Like many teenagers, Jeff didn't talk about everything going on in his life. Smitty had to ask around to learn there was drama in Jeff's home. An aunt in another state had a drug problem, so her three kids had moved into the house. It was an enormous distraction. Smitty had a feeling it explained the gap between the youngster's SAT scores and his grades. Jeff could focus on a test in a hushed site, but not on homework in a chaotic house.

Not every college counselor delved into such details, but Smitty felt that learning such secrets, and helping kids cope with them, was the essence of his job at Oyster Bay High.

TWO

Who Am I?

Toward the end of another too warm September day, as the eighth-period students sat around the long table in the Essay Writing for College class, Smitty loosened them up by asking what careers they were considering.

"I want to be a doctor," a girl said.

"A psychiatrist," said the valedictorian, Layla.

"I want to be a—an astronomy person," said the class clown, "whatever that's called."

"A psychologist," said a cheerful girl named Allyson Frankel. "Sort of like a psychiatrist."

Smitty knew Allyson to be a driven student. She was one of the kids he considered a special project.

It was the third day of the school year and already Allyson had chosen colleges and begun her application essays. Many counselors would applaud that, but Smitty urged the kids to hold back a bit longer. He felt they should think hard about what they wanted from college before rushing to apply. Besides, a guidance staff can't properly guide kids they don't yet fully know.

Over the decades, Smitty had seen too many seventeen-year-olds make hasty decisions, celebrate an acceptance, send in their deposit, and eventually regret it. He knew the feeling all too well. Years ago he'd done the same thing.

"Does everyone understand the difference between a psychiatrist and a psychologist?" Smitty asked. "A psychiatrist goes to medical school, but a psychologist doesn't."

Then Smitty asked Allyson what kind of psychologist she wanted to be. "A researcher? A counselor with a private practice?"

"Doing art therapy," she said. "Helping kids."

In many ways, Allyson was the opposite of Jeff, one of Smitty's other "projects." He was in the lower half of the class, she was near the top, with an A average. He came off as scattered, she was well organized. While Jeff frustrated some of his teachers, Allyson delighted hers. Because Smitty lived with Kathi Reilly, he heard about kids like Allyson. Kathi had taught Allyson in eleventh grade honors English, and said she was the kind of kid who read *Siddhartha* for fun. Now, also on her own, Allyson had rushed ahead of the pack in her college quest.

By this first week of senior year, she had narrowed her search to ten schools. Her sister was a senior at Emory and loved it, which put it high on Allyson's list. She also liked the University of Michigan.

But she was self-aware enough to see a problem with her chances at those colleges. As she put it: "Statistically I'm qualified, but my demographic, a white Jewish girl from Long Island, isn't exactly unique."

She saw that having qualifying scores isn't enough if you don't stand out in your region. It might be different if she was applying from North Dakota with her identical record. But she wasn't.

Some kids were fun to work with as they applied to college, while others were frustrating; Smitty had no doubt Chelsea Flynn would be both.

She was a talented writer and photographer with what Smitty called "an artist's personality." That meant she did creative work, though not exactly by deadline. Kathi, who had taught her honors English in eleventh grade, agreed. Chelsea turned in her essays late, but they were usually among the best in the class.

Smitty called Chelsea "effervescent" because she seemed to always be bubbling about something. "I saw the most amazing performance art in the city," she'd tell him while passing in the hallway, then she'd float away.

Smitty felt that each student's list of colleges should share a theme. If a kid liked small liberal arts schools, that's where he should apply, just as a "rah-rah" kid should keep a focus on big schools with giant football stadiums. He had no problem with a small-school applicant including some state universities in case money proved tight. But Smitty didn't believe in applying scattershot to schools that had nothing in common. And he thought there was such a thing as too long a list.

It had become common for students in America to apply to a dozen or more colleges. Smitty knew of a boy at John F. Kennedy High on the South Shore who had applied to thirty-four the previous year. At sixty dollars per app, it likely cost his family more than two thousand dollars just to send in the packets. That's over-the-top and, worse, it blurred a student's focus. With so many applications, how could you do each one well? And with so many choices, could you really have a clear idea of where you wanted to go?

Chelsea was one of those kids prone to mixing it up because she couldn't decide. She was interested in Tulane in the South and Middlebury in the North. She liked the way the College of Charleston was part of a city and the way Skidmore was near the Adirondack Mountains. She could see herself at NYU, the ultimate urban campus, but she was also interested in Alabama's Spring Hill College, on the Gulf Coast. Smitty had no idea where Chelsea would ultimately apply. He expected she would approach her applications as she did her class assignments—she'd do a fantastic job, at the last minute.

R iana Tyson sat against a side wall during the first few days of Essay Writing for College, keeping to herself and barely saying a word. It's one reason Smitty chose to work with her. She was an accomplished girl, but quiet in class, always staying under the radar, and the contrast intrigued him. She was one of only three seniors who were African American, another twist that made him want to look out for her.

Riana had a 93.4 average. That might have been an impressive GPA at Oyster Bay thirty years before, but not now. Smitty had watched over time as college pressure pushed more kids to compete hard academically, and grades inflated. It had gotten to a point where the school board decided to make Oyster Bay a "no-ranking" institution. That meant Smitty would tell colleges only who was in first and second place—the valedictorian and salutatorian. The rest were identified as first quintile, second quintile, and so on. Smitty liked the idea. With so many Oyster Bay students bunched closely in grade average, he didn't think it fair that a kid should be ranked, say, fifteenth if she was only a few decimals behind a kid who was fifth.

More important, Smitty felt rankings fed the unhealthy trend to define kids by statistics. Riana, for example, would have been 41st of Oyster Bay's 109 seniors, which might have counted against her. Yet Smitty knew that in her quiet way, she could be a leader. The school had two well-regarded clubs called SADD and Undecided. The first, Students Against Destructive Decisions, put on plays and displays to warn kids against drugs, drinking, and smoking. Undecided gave students a safe place to talk about their lives. Riana was president of both.

Before senior year started, she had stopped by to see Smitty. She'd signed up for Advanced Placement government and now surprised him by saying she wanted to take Advanced Placement statistics with a demanding teacher. Smitty approved. He urged her to take AP calculus, too.

Riana agreed.

Smitty had seen her coast through classes. Was she truly ready to step up this way? He hoped so, but did she know what she was getting herself into? She was taking a fourth AP class, physics. He warned her it would be a grueling senior year.

"Learning is easy," she told him. "I don't need to study a lot. I figure stuff out."

Smitty made his point again: "This is going to be quite a change in your life. You have a schedule now, my dear, that's going to require you to study."

Room 207, where Essay Writing for College met, was long and narrow, with scarred wooden floors. The room had a whiteboard up front and a gray desk piled with binders stuffed with previous application essays. Along the walls, there were twenty-two computers to help students search for colleges, write résumés, and work on compositions.

The tall windows looked out over the school's sloping front lawn. Beyond that was Main Street, and then three blocks of Colonials and gracious Victorians. From the classroom, you could see over those roofs to Oyster Bay's harbor and the Long Island Sound.

Kathi would start the class by talking around the conference table, then direct students to the computers. A few pecked at sports scores and celebrity sites. To the students' displeasure, the computers blocked e-mail and instant messaging.

Smitty stopped by on most days. True to his Maine upbringing, the kids saw, he was bothered by the late-summer humidity. He'd often fuss with the settings of two large air conditioners. Then Kathi, who grew up by the beach on Long Island and loved hot weather, would complain that the room was too chilly. "Can somebody turn those things down?" she'd call out. The temperature-control drama was a welcome distraction for students looking for a break from all the talk of essays, acceptances, and rejections.

By the end of the first week of school, Kathi handed back the essay to Kasper, the boy whose father had been killed by a train. Kasper appeared to be doing well despite the trauma. He seemed emotionally centered, and was still known for his ready laugh. Kathi knew she didn't need to be polite.

"You have a problem with the essay?" Kasper asked.

"The problem is—the problem is everything," she said. "This is basically a list of your accomplishments. It's got no voice. It's got no point."

"I guess you want me to rewrite it."

"That'd be a good idea," Kathi said.

She thought for a moment. "Can I ask you a favor?"

Kasper nodded.

"Can I keep it and use it as an example of what *not* to do?"

There was a brief pause. Then Kasper flashed his broad smile.

"I'd be flattered," he said.

B y most measures—test scores, grades, science awards—the class of 2008 was not as strong as the previous few at Oyster Bay High. This year, Smitty felt only a couple of kids had a great chance at getting into Ivy League schools. One was Colin, a star on a local crew team, who was being recruited by Princeton, Yale, and Dartmouth. His 1460 combined SAT score was the highest in the class. The other was Lee Kim. Lee's 1410 score was tied for third highest. He spoke Korean with his parents, and was such a good singer that he was selected an All Eastern States soloist, one of only three in the school's history.

During the spring of his junior year, Lee had come to Smitty to talk about college. He liked the University of Chicago, where his older brother was studying. A few weeks later, though, Lee said he wanted to go to Oxford University.

"Are you trying to test me?" Smitty said. He'd been a guidance counselor since the Nixon administration, and in all those years no one had ever mentioned Oxford.

When Lee next returned, he'd changed his mind. His father had gone on the Internet and found another school: Deep Springs.

"Deep *what?*" Smitty asked. He knew hundreds of colleges, but had no idea where Deep Springs was. As he went online to look, he called a buddy who worked as a private admissions consultant and kept track of offbeat colleges. "I've got one for you," Smitty said. "Deep Springs."

"Small two-year school in California, all male, founded by some industrialist," his friend replied. "A working ranch. Less than thirty kids, all on full scholarship. Superb students, very high SAT scores. Sort of a feeder for the Ivy League."

Deep Springs students did chores in the early mornings and after classes, spent afternoons repairing fences, working in alfalfa fields, or insulating pipes. "There are less romantic jobs," the Web site explained, "that entail spending the day in the office or scrubbing toilets."

Just a few weeks before, Lee Kim had been talking about the oldest university in the English-speaking world, and now a ranch school where kids toiled in alfalfa fields. Smitty was starting to think that finding the right college for Lee, brilliant as he might be, was going to be a challenge.

. . .

E ach time he checked in with these five students—Jeff, Allyson, Lee, Chelsea, and Riana—Smitty made sure he didn't just talk college. He asked Allyson about a speed-reading course she'd taken. He debriefed Chelsea about her museum trips. He inquired about Lee's progress practicing "Ol' Man River" for a school concert. With Jeff and Riana, Smitty chatted about the struggling New York Jets. It wasn't just idle chatter. In a way, those talks were about college, too. In picking the right school, it helped to know students' scores, but it helped far more to get to know who they really were.

THREE

BWRK

Name: Allyson Frankel
Weighted GPA: 101.2—15th in the class of 109
SAT: 680 critical reading + 590 math = 1270 composite
ACT: 29

Emory or Michigan?

As Allyson Frankel sat in the wooden visitor's chair in Smitty's office, she said she needed help thinking about her two top choices. On one hand, Emory seemed the natural place for her. She'd traveled there a half dozen times to see her sister and had grown comfortable with its Atlanta campus. But she was also intrigued with the University of Michigan. It was more an unknown—she'd seen Ann Arbor only briefly. Still, she'd liked what she saw very much.

Allyson's sister gave some advice about Emory. Apply early decision, she said. The odds were better that way—especially for a girl from New

York. The campus was full of such kids, her sister said, and far more of them would be competing in the April pool than during ED. Allyson didn't know what to do. What if she ultimately decided Michigan was the right place? If she got into Emory early, she'd have to withdraw all her other applications immediately.

Allyson asked Smitty what he thought.

He decided to make her back up a bit, answering with questions of his own.

"Have you decided that you want to go away? You feel good being a plane trip from home?"

Allyson said she'd spent her whole life in Oyster Bay, and was ready for a change. She'd enjoyed going out of state to summer camp and meeting kids from all over.

"College is when you get to learn the most about yourself," she said, "and you learn the most about yourself when you're around people that are different."

Smitty said it was refreshing to hear that from a youngster. "So tell me more about your two favorite campuses."

Allyson had been to classes, meals, and parties at Emory. Her sister had found great friends and great professors. Allyson smiled and added: a great boyfriend, too.

"I've kind of lived the Emory experience vicariously," she told Smitty. "I know all the scenes, all the programs." But recently she'd been thinking that could be a negative.

"I might be ready for something new," she mused.

Smitty didn't like to tell kids what to do. This was a process of self-discovery, and he felt he should lead kids to find answers. He turned the conversation to Michigan. How did the school get on her radar? And why did she think Michigan could be the place?

Over the summer, Allyson had taken courses at a program at the University of Wisconsin. On weekends, they took kids on bus tours of the region's Big Ten campuses.

Smitty asked her to tell him about each one.

"Indiana was good," she said, "but it wasn't my favorite. It might get dull after a couple of years. Ohio State impressed me, but I didn't see myself there. Northwestern is gorgeous, but I think it's too intense, too competitive."

Then, why Michigan?

"Michigan just looked amazing," Allyson said. She admitted it was a surface impression—her tour bus didn't have much time so they merely drove through the campus.

Smitty had no problem with that. In a college search, liking the look of a place is a key factor, and can often lead to the right fit. That's why college visits—even brief ones—are essential. You can be intrigued with a school from afar, but see it differently once you arrive on campus.

He asked her to elaborate.

Looking out the bus window that day, Allyson explained, she saw students playing catch on big lawns, drinking coffee on benches, and reading by ivy-covered buildings. "It was the way I'd always imagined college," she said.

She also loved Michigan's big size: 200 majors; 900 student associations, and freshmen from more than 1,600 high schools. After seventeen years in a small suburb, she was ready for a more expansive world.

Allyson had learned details about the school by talking with friends of friends at Michigan, and going online to read students' comments at sites like www.CollegeConfidential.com and www.theU.com. Everyone raved about the social life and academics. Michigan had a thriving sorority scene, and Allyson thought she might like to join it.

Allyson's family had a tradition of going to good colleges. Her grandparents had attended NYU, Cornell, Penn, and SUNY Oneonta. Her parents had met at Boston University. Her oldest sister graduated from BU.

Smitty asked if Allyson had been thinking about BU.

She had been. For now, she'd included BU out of family loyalty, although it seemed too urban.

Her list had ten schools:

University of Michigan
Emory
Lehigh
University of Wisconsin
Tulane
Indiana University
University of Miami
Penn State
George Washington
Boston University

Michigan had rolling admissions, so they would read and decide on her application in the order it was received. If she was going to apply, she thought she should do so quickly. But she hadn't made up her mind yet.

It was time to wrap up. Smitty told her she was doing a good job weighing priorities so far. She thanked him and left, realizing that he hadn't answered the question she had come there to ask: Emory or Michigan?

She wondered if he'd gotten sidetracked or if maybe avoided answering on purpose.

Smitty's office was at the back of what could be called the guidance cave, at the rear of the school away from natural light. It was a calming suite of rooms, with a jar of Hershey's Kisses at the entrance and a goldfish aquarium inside. The department secretary, Blossom, sat in the middle. The two younger counselors, both women in their twenties, called themselves "Smitty's angels."

Smitty's own office had a desk, a round table, a file cabinet, two crowded bookshelves, and four wooden chairs. Stacks of transcripts and essays rose higher as deadlines approached—November 1 and 15 for early apps and January 1 and 15 for most others. The piles would fall as the dates passed. There was just enough space between the piles to put down his lunch, almost always a banana and two oranges.

His office walls had artwork from students and a calendar featuring twelve photos of his grandson. At eye level, he displayed three of his favorite keepsakes. One was his father's diploma from Columbia University's Teachers College. The second was a United Negro College Fund plaque honoring Smitty for starting a college fair for black students on Long Island. The third was a more personal plaque. It was from a family whose children he'd helped. It thanked him for being "a person who truly makes a positive difference in this world."

Smitty's office lacked the usual college posters of joyful students sitting in a sun-speckled quad. He didn't want youngsters feeling pressure to live up to some idealized image of college. On his round meeting table this day, he had a coffee mug from the University of Chicago. It was one of dozens of mugs sent to him over the years by former students. Atop one bookshelf sat a framed photo of a girl in a cap and gown at Oyster Bay's graduation eight years earlier. He kept it as a reminder of his need to always do better. She'd been shut out of every college she applied to. In Smitty's eyes, if a student is rejected everywhere, it's in part a failure of the counseling staff to ensure the right target schools. Smitty liked that term more than "safety schools," which implied you were merely settling for something. "That incident," he often said with a grimace, "is something I don't ever want to repeat."

Smitty wasn't an especially eloquent speaker. His strength was drawing kids out, listening carefully, and leading them to their own conclusions.

His friend Matt Brown, a school social worker, was often better at articulating Smitty's mission than Smitty himself. The two had met when Smitty came to Oyster Bay High for a job interview in 1999, and had talked to each other almost every workday since.

"Smitty becomes a father figure to many of the kids," Matt said. "He has all the concern, all the personal investment, that a parent should have, but he also draws the line and looks objectively as he decides what makes sense for a kid."

Matt's own son and daughter had attended a school district that boasted of its emphasis on the college admissions process, yet when the teachers looked at application essays, they focused on spelling and grammar rather than on helping Matt's kids find their voices.

"Smitty," said Matt, "is interested in reading between the lines to find out what's happening in someone's heart."

As a social worker, Matt often dealt with students stressed by the college chase. He felt high schools pushed families too hard through the process. In district after district, he'd seen an increasing obsession with two words: *getting in*. Parents and kids needed to see it the way Smitty did, in a broader context.

Matt described Smitty's outlook this way: "It's about reflecting on where you've been and how that impacts where you're going."

While some counselors pressed students to master the tricks of admission, Smitty was among those who got kids to first look at themselves. If you view college through that lens, Matt felt, you'll have a better chance to chart a meaningful path once you get there.

During a lull between appointments, Smitty reviewed Allyson's file. He considered whether she could get into Emory with so many similar applicants in the pool. She'd gotten a composite ACT score of 29 out of

36, a bit under the 30–33 range Emory considered its standard. He looked at Allyson's SATs. Her composite for reading and math, 1270, was low for Emory, whose range was 1300–1470.

Smitty put less stock in the third part of the SAT, the writing test. He felt a timed writing sample of twenty-five minutes was far from an ideal predictor of performance in college, where students had days to revise a paper. The kind of work the kids did in his Essay Writing for College class was more relevant, which is why he and Kathi had given it that name.

Smitty knew that many colleges, including Emory and Michigan, merely glanced at the SAT writing scores. In Allyson's case, that was unfortunate. She had gotten an impressive 750.

As for Michigan, Smitty had seen its dean of admissions, Ted Spencer, speak at conferences, where he of course said the school did its best to find the right kids. Smitty liked him, but knew that with twenty-nine thousand applications pouring in each year, Michigan had limited time for each folder. While he felt Allyson had a better chance at Michigan, it wasn't guaranteed.

As he sat there pondering, Smitty was now up against the pragmatic side of being a college counselor. As much as he was about youngsters looking within themselves, Gwyeth Smith Jr. was also charged with getting students accepted, and he took that seriously. He opposed finagling kids into schools that were over their heads, but if it was the right place, he would do all he could to close the deal.

In selling Allyson Frankel to Michigan or Emory, Smitty knew he had to stress something beyond scores and grades. When it came to kids on the cusp, colleges look for a hook—a legacy, an athletic talent, perhaps an underrepresented group. Allyson was what many admissions offices call a BWRK—a bright, well-rounded kid. That would help, but she'd need more. One thing that came to Smitty's mind was "Jammin' for Justice," a memorable event she organized junior year, pulling together a band and selling T-shirts to raise forty-five hundred dollars for Darfur refugees. It showed social conscience, but in a creative way that would add to a college community. It also showed an entrepreneur's touch.

As he considered how to write her recommendation, he jotted down these thoughts. This was a case, he felt, where if he did his job well, he might make the difference.

FOUR

"When Everybody Is Special, Nobody Is Special"

Name: Lee Kim
Weighted GPA: 103.2—12th in the class of 109
SAT: 680 critical reading + 730 math = 1410 composite
ACT: 31

If any Oyster Bay student had been groomed for the most prestigious colleges, it was Lee Kim. Not only did he have the third-best SATs in his class, he also spoke Korean, and played six instruments well. He'd started learning the violin at age four, guitar at seven, clarinet at nine, saxophone at ten, cello at fifteen, and piano in between. He joked that his musical record wasn't perfect—he quit the harmonica after one lesson.

Lee was tall, fine-boned, and handsome. When he dressed for performances, he looked as if he'd been born in black tie. But Lee's inner identity wasn't simply a musician. He was a boy trying to balance the pressure to overachieve with a yearning to go his own way.

From a young age, Lee rarely had a minute free. After school and on Saturdays, he'd attended enrichment classes in math, science, and Korean. He took his first practice SAT in sixth grade—years earlier than most kids. On Sundays, he was an altar boy at a Catholic church.

His father and mother had gone to college in Korea then emigrated to New York, where Lee was born. His dad found work in a funeral home, arriving in the morning before other employees and staying later at night. He soon bought the business, and within a few years owned two other funeral homes. Lee admired his dad's work ethic, and was proud that after 9/11 his dad donated services to victims.

Lee's older sister had gone to a top college in Korea. His older brother was such a standout at Oyster Bay High that his parents transferred Lee to a Catholic school so he wouldn't be in his sibling's shadow. But then, in the middle of tenth grade, Lee abruptly returned to Oyster Bay High. There were whispers that he must have gotten in trouble. Someone started a rumor that he'd cursed out a coach. Lee heard the gossip, but didn't talk about what happened.

Some teachers told Smitty that Lee had come back with an attitude, acting like he was above public school. He charged through the halls ignoring everyone else, they said, as if he were an executive on his way to a board meeting.

What appeared to be arrogance was a front. Lee's secret truth was that despite his achievements, he felt conflicted. In part, it was about religion. He'd been brought up Catholic, attending church youth groups. He'd even gone on missions to Bosnia, Peru, and Mexico. Lately, though, he'd been questioning whether religion helped people or hurt them.

Mostly, Lee wrestled with expectations. He'd been raised to be what he referred to as a "good son." This role was symbolized by a New Year's tradition in which he bowed before family elders, spoke of his appreciation of them, then received gifts from them. In his case, as a good son, he was supposed to go to college and return to take over the family funeral business. Increasingly, though, Lee wanted to follow his own course, just as his parents had done when they emigrated from Korea. Some days he wanted to make a lot of money. Others he thought about creating a nonprofit to help the poor help themselves. He'd seen a need for that during his missions overseas. Or maybe he'd start a small company, get married, and just concentrate on his own family. All he knew was that he felt the weight of everyone else's expectations.

Lee was at a point where he no longer knew where his parents' dreams stopped and his own started. At times, he felt that no matter how much he did, it was hard to distinguish himself. At Korean school on Saturday, he'd look around the room and see dozens of kids who were accomplished at science, math, music, and art. "They're all going to the special talent camps or research camps, so everybody is brought up to a high level," he would explain. "When everybody is special, nobody is special."

Just as Allyson worried about being dismissed as another Jewish kid from Long Island, Lee assumed admissions offices would see him as one more Korean American high achiever. Some of his Asian friends felt that colleges practiced academic discrimination, holding them to a higher standard. Lee said he didn't spend a lot of time agonizing over issues like that. There was no point worrying about something out of your control.

Lee could tell that Mr. Smith and Ms. Reilly thought he wasn't focusing enough on his applications, but they didn't understand. Lee found the application procedure unseemly. He felt college admissions departments fixated on facts and scores but failed to see the whole person. As for the process of picking schools, Lee couldn't get excited about it. Really, what made one university better than another? It seemed to Lee that if you worked hard at college, you'd learn something—but the work you put in mattered more than the name on the gates. He didn't spend much time thinking about the pecking order of schools, nor did he look at College Confidential or other such Web sites.

His list came from his parents asking their friends where Lee "should" apply. So far they'd come up with five of the eight Ivy League campuses, along with Swarthmore, Vanderbilt, Amherst, Williams, and Stanford. It wasn't his list, but at times Lee admitted that it might be nice to get an acceptance from Princeton or Yale. It would be a tribute to the journey his family had made in a single generation.

Some mornings in the first-period Essay Writing for College class, while most other kids were focused on applications, Lee would sit with Dominique, the would-be actress, and talk about anything other than colleges and essays. One day he told her he'd been thinking about enlisting in the military.

She looked at him in surprise.

"I need the discipline," he said.

Many folks would have considered Lee Kim among the most disciplined kids in the class. But he worried he didn't have his father's work ethic. That, he sensed, was something they couldn't teach you in college.

For much of the twentieth century, most Oyster Bay residents had done fine without college degrees. There had been plenty of jobs for carpenters, nurses, and shop clerks. Those who did continue with school often chose community colleges or near by campuses. That changed in the late 1980s and 1990s as affluent professionals bought houses in Oyster Bay. By 1999, the school board thought more students should be aiming for the country's best colleges, like their peers in neighboring districts. The board began a search for a guidance director who could help.

When Smitty interviewed for the job, Oyster Bay's principal asked how he would apply the lessons of a popular book, *A Is for Admission,* by a former Dartmouth admissions officer. The book promised to share the secret formula—the "Academic Index"—used by the Ivy schools to evaluate candidates. Smitty said he avoided talk about a formula, because it led parents to believe that everything came down to numbers.

He'd spent enough time with admissions deans to know the game was more intuitive than outsiders realized. Transcripts and scores mattered, of course, but he argued that admissions reps were often swayed by a kid's personal narrative.

In the interview, Smitty agreed that the guidance office needed to get Oyster Bay's kids into good schools. But he had an approach he considered more effective than a "secret formula."

He described seven principles.

First, he thought students should take the high school's most demanding courses, and a counselor should find other options at nearby two- or four-year colleges.

Second, counselors needed to get to know kids and their families personally—well enough to guide them toward the right schools.

Third, a counselor had to be blunt with parents shooting too high, and candid with college admissions staffs about a kid's pros and cons. Overselling a student could hurt the credibility of a counselor or push someone into a college that was too rigorous.

Fourth, he told students to make a "hit list," not of ideal or prestigious colleges but of those where they could truly see themselves.

Fifth, he urged youngsters to take both the ACT and the SAT exams, because individual test-taking styles favored one or the other.

Sixth, he insisted that the school district pay for intensive prep courses so that middle- and working-class students could be on the same playing field as the rich.

Finally, he pushed students to rewrite their essays as many times as it took to make the pieces outstanding. He knew many kids settled for mediocrity, but Smitty believed an essay could make or break a qualified applicant's chances.

Smitty sensed that his skeptical remarks about *A Is for Admission* had not endeared him to the search committee. He left the interview assuming he'd sabotaged his chance of getting the job. He hadn't. They hired him.

He quickly started to put his ideas into practice. Guidance directors at some schools spent their time managing colleagues, but Smitty took on a caseload of seniors. He soon convinced the board to hire a test-prep coach. It paid off. In the next two years, Oyster Bay's average SAT score climbed eighty points. He doubled the number of students taking the ACT, which hadn't been popular with New Yorkers. Finally, he and Kathi launched their essay-writing course.

In some other areas, Smitty was less successful. He found it difficult to convince Oyster Bay students to expand the narrow band of schools they'd been applying to. The top students looked at the Ivy League and well-known names in the Boston–Washington corridor, along with North-western, Duke, UNC, and UVA. Occasionally, they considered Berkeley or USC, but largely ignored the "flyover" states as well as the so-called Little Ivies, such as Amherst, Williams, and Wesleyan. The next tier of students looked at competitive campuses from BU to George Washington University, along with a few reliable places, like the University of Delaware—most also in the Northeast or mid-Atlantic.

Even if students planned to return to live on Long Island, Smitty urged them to spend four years away. For students who liked the small-town feel of Oyster Bay, he stressed that Pennsylvania had gems such as Muhlenberg, Allegheny, and Franklin & Marshall; Ohio had Oberlin, Denison, Wooster, Kenyon, and Miami University; Iowa had Grinnell; Minnesota had Carleton and Macalester; Oregon had Reed and Lewis & Clark; North Carolina had Elon. Smitty often touted his home state, Maine, with Colby, Bates, and Bowdoin. For that matter, upstate New York offered Hamilton, Hobart, and William Smith—schools that Oyster Bay kids could reach in a little more time than it took to drive out to the Hamptons in rush hour traffic.

To coax students to explore the country, Smitty kept a copy of the *Official Airline Guide,* the *OAG,* next to his computer. He liked to show parents the "Jet Blue effect," which made places like Eckerd College in Florida, Trinity University in Texas, and Furman in South Carolina accessible by flights on no-frills carriers.

But he didn't have a lot of luck: The majority of Oyster Bay students went to college within a hundred miles of home. Smitty wished more were willing to try the unknown.

Every so often, someone in room 207 would grow intrigued with a far-away school. One morning, a boy with dark hair down to his eyes began to check out the Web site of Bond University in Australia, which called itself the "college down under."

"That's where I want to go," the boy announced.

One of the other kids challenged him: He'd hardly been south of the Long Island Expressway, and now he was going to college halfway around the world?

He demurred. Well, he would at least talk to his parents about it.

Smitty liked this early stage of the college search because it allowed teenagers to dream. He encouraged them to scan the room's guidebooks, go to college fairs, and cull suggestions from Web sites.

He picked out particular kids he hoped might break away from the Northeast, like Jeff Sanders's girlfriend, Jenna. She would need considerable financial aid. It got Smitty thinking about Duke and Vanderbilt, tough schools but ones with money as well as a soft spot for a kid with a great story.

Jenna's father was a bayman, and her mother a nurse. Neither had a degree from a four-year college, and yet Jenna had become the second-ranked student in her class. She'd made a spreadsheet of her top choices, Columbia, Brown, NYU, and Barnard. She filled the columns with eighteen factors, from the number of undergrads to the application fee. It was one of the best-organized summaries Smitty had seen a student put together. Soon after, Jenna and her parents spent a day visiting the Manhattan campuses. She came back and told Smitty that Columbia and NYU were too intense, but she loved Columbia's sister school, Barnard, alma mater of successful women from Margaret Mead to Martha Stewart. She planned to apply early decision.

A part of Smitty was disappointed that she wouldn't consider something farther away, but he didn't say so. Barnard was a great school, known as the "side door to the Ivy League." If Jenna needed to keep close ties to home, then that's who she was.

The valedictorian, Layla, was more daring. She'd been to India, Russia, and Japan with her mother, and was clear about her career plans. She wanted to find a great premed program and then study psychiatry. She jotted her hit list in a black journal. A few weeks into the school year, she had fifteen choices, and she wasn't done.

Columbia

Barnard

University of Miami—medical program

Siena College—medical program

Villanova—medical program

Vassar

McGill

Emory

Stony Brook—honors program

George Washington University—medical program

Boston University

NYU

Brown

University of Rochester—medical program

Harvard

The year's most adventurous applicant appeared to be Lee Kim. His college choices spanned three countries: Oxford in England; McGill in Canada; and in the United States, everything from Yale to Deep Springs. Smitty found Lee's reasoning rather shaky. Explaining Oxford, which he'd never visited, Lee said simply, "It's across the pond, far away from my parents. It's in Europe, so it's automatically cool."

One morning in mid-September, Smitty called Lee in for a college talk. Lee said he could see himself at Oxford, but his father still liked Deep Springs, as he had the previous spring. "My dad thinks the experience would be good," Lee said. "He's very much more about the experience than the prestige. My mom is into prestige." That, he added, is why he'd included Yale, Princeton, Amherst, and Williams on his list. As for the aspirations of Lee's father, Smitty now knew Deep Springs regularly sent its young men to the Ivies.

"What about you?" Smitty said.

"Any of those places is okay."

"Can you be more specific? Do you want a Norman Rockwell town? A big city? Small city?"

"Any big or small city that's away from home."

"Let's take a different approach: What do you want to study?"

Here, Lee was definitive: "Business. At the bottom of everything is business."

Smitty asked if Lee had heard of any schools with noted undergraduate business programs. Lee mentioned two, the Wharton School at Penn and the Stern School at New York University, but admitted that he didn't know much about them.

"I don't see myself at any one college specifically," he said. "I want to go away from home." That seemed to be his top goal.

Then he added, "I'm going to apply to Harvard, too."

"Harvard doesn't have a business major for undergrads," said Smitty.

"I know, but it's Harvard."

It made Smitty realize that Lee wasn't entirely above his parents' priorities. Still, Smitty felt Lee needed to face reality. While his 1410 on the SATs stood out at Oyster Bay, it wasn't a door opener for the top schools on his list. Almost anyone would be glad to have his 103.2 grade point average, but that could be better, too. Oyster Bay used weighted averages, adding points for Advanced Placement courses, so it wasn't uncommon for the first fifteen kids in the senior class to have averages well over 100.

Smitty warned Lee that his first-quarter grades from senior year mattered because competitive schools would compare him to his peers. "You need to perform, and perform at a very high level," Smitty said.

He also suggested that Lee take the SAT one more time. Lee's grades suggested his boards could be higher.

Although Lee didn't mention it to anyone, he had an incentive to try again. During junior year, his father had promised him a used minivan if he got a total score of 2100 on critical reading, math, and writing. If he could boost the score to 2200, he'd get a used convertible. If he hit the reading, math, and writing trifecta—a perfect 2400—he could pick out any new car he wanted. He'd squeaked by the first target, with a 2120, and had the used Dodge Grand Caravan to show for it.

If he got the perfect score, he knew which car he'd ask for: a Tesla Roadster—the ultimate sports car with a carbon fiber body and a lithium-ion battery pack. It listed for about $100,000. That broke down to $42 for every single point on the perfect SATs.

Smitty wasn't sure yet what to make of Lee Kim. The boy wanted to go his own way, and yet he didn't. Some people spent decades figuring out this question. Smitty wasn't sure Lee could resolve it by May 1, the deadline for paying a deposit for freshman year.

FIVE

"You're Lost Before You've Started"

Name: Chelsea Flynn

Weighted GPA: 99.5—20th in the class of 109

SAT: 650 critical reading + 650 math = 1300 composite

ACT: not taken

Chelsea Flynn collapsed into a chair in her guidance counselor's office. First period had already started. "Before you say anything about me being late, Mr. Smith," she declared, "I have to tell you that I am *sooo* stressed."

Of Smitty's special projects, she was his artsy one, yet she was driven, too.

Chelsea was taking nine straight forty-two-minute classes in a row every day and playing varsity soccer. After that, she had a job at a test-prep center. She had once had a grand ambition to write a novel before graduation—she hadn't been sure about what—but now was simply trying to keep up with her daily schedule. She told Smitty she had no free time left, and was falling behind.

"Which is my downfall," she added, "because when I'm behind I get stressed."

"How do you deal with that?" Smitty said.

"I write to deal with the stress. I write every day."

"That's cathartic."

"And I have panic attacks."

Chelsea's hair was in a French braid with blond wisps sticking out. She wore skinny jeans, a black scoop-neck top, a narrow blue scarf, and green flats. She somehow managed to look disheveled and fashionable at the same time.

She told Smitty of her to-do list: She had to study for the SAT II subject tests in French and English. She needed to pull together a portfolio to show to college art programs. She wanted to visit more campuses, which meant missing classes and getting even more stressed.

"I just want to fast-forward to April, and find out where I'm going to college," she said.

Smitty felt his job right now was to help Chelsea slow down and find some satisfaction in the application process.

"What kind of school do you see yourself at?" Smitty said. "City? Suburban?"

"No idea."

"Close to home or far away?"

"I used to think I wanted to be in New England because I know what it's like. My uncle lives in Vermont and I go snowboarding there."

She said she liked UVM but suspected it was too cold to spend four years there.

Smitty changed his tack. "For now, forget about *where* you want to go to college. *Why* do you want to go?"

Chelsea hoped to one day be a photographer, author, or art teacher. She wanted a school that would inspire her to pursue those things, and make it easy to do so late into the night, as was her style.

Like Allyson, Chelsea enjoyed English, social studies, and art. They were different in many ways, however. Allyson lived in a modern home in a suburban development. Her bedroom, painted green, was neatly arranged. Chelsea, on the other hand, lived in a rambling house in the old neighborhood next to the school, her room filled with piles of clothes and books. Allyson drove an Audi; Chelsea borrowed her mother's Prius hybrid.

The two girls approached the college hunt differently, too. Allyson had all but narrowed her search to two choices; Chelsea kept finding new schools that interested her. Allyson was finishing her essays, while Chelsea admitted she didn't know what the Common App was until a few days earlier. She knew she was behind, and not just in her college search.

"My mom always says if you don't know where you're going, you're lost before you've started," she told her guidance counselor. "I have no idea what I'm doing at all."

One positive was that she had seen a number of campuses. Her sister had been a senior at Oyster Bay High the year before, and Chelsea had tagged along on college visits. While her sister checked out the University of North Carolina at Chapel Hill, Chelsea had taken a side trip to the College of Charleston, South Carolina. She thought UNC was too big but liked Charleston.

In August, she'd gone with a friend to visit three colleges in Maine. "Colby and Bates were too remote," she said. But she liked Bowdoin.

"I'm glad, my dear," said Smitty. "That's where I grew up."

"They talked a lot about how the classes are only part of your learning," she said of Bowdoin. "How much they value athletics and social life. I liked that they addressed it."

"I know the admissions director," Smitty told her. "A good man. Used to work at Vandy. Gets so involved with the applicants that he goes to lunch with them when they become students. That tells you something about Bowdoin."

But Chelsea was torn. She wondered if a city campus would be more invigorating for someone like her, a night owl who needed the stimulation of artists and writers. She'd heard that Brown was a good place for a writer, but she didn't know if she could get in.

Smitty reminded Chelsea that she wasn't the first in her family to be looking at very different places. Her own sister had liked the University of Vermont and Dartmouth before happily going to McGill.

"You have some time to figure this out," Smitty told Chelsea. "But not too long, my dear. It's one thing to turn in an essay late to Ms. Reilly. It's another to convince an admissions office to excuse you when you missed their deadline."

Smitty was diligent about warning kids to plan carefully, but he'd made a few mistakes of his own in his career. One of the worst happened after he'd taken time off from counseling to do more lucrative work for a private education company. He returned to counseling in the 1999–2000 term, his first year at Oyster Bay. One of the seniors was a good student, an editor of the school paper, and a field hockey player. She'd applied to seven colleges including Middlebury, Wesleyan, and Colgate. But her assigned counselor hadn't made sure she had backup schools. By mid-April, she had been shut out by all seven. As the director of a small department, Smitty felt personally responsible.

It was a crisis. He called the girl's parents to his office to help them make a new hit list, including several colleges where he had good contacts—critical when trying to work a deal after acceptances were sent out.

Smitty picked up the phone, telling his contacts, "I've got a problem that involves a fabulous youngster." Some schools barred their admissions officers from taking calls from private consultants but allowed them to talk to school counselors. It also helped that students lately were applying to so many places that quite a few schools were overestimating their yields. In a few days he managed to find the girl a spot at Franklin & Marshall in Pennsylvania, with a $7,500 per year presidential scholarship.

Chelsea updated Smitty on her college search every few days. She was interested in Middlebury, despite the long winters. She was intrigued by the writing classes at NYU. She could see herself at New Paltz, a SUNY school with an artsy reputation. She liked to exhaustively weigh all possibilities.

"I'm pretty indecisive," she said. "But then when I make a decision I'm sure of it."

Smitty could tell when Chelsea was feeling less stressed. When he passed her in the hallway, she'd tell him of her latest adventures: "Hi, Mr. Smith! I saw Andy Warhol's stuff at MoMA!" . . . "I went to a play in SoHo" . . . "I'm reading *Crime and Punishment* for Ms. Reilly, and it's the best!"

Smitty liked such "Chelsea moments." She was one of those kids who treated high school as if it were college—she drew on every resource around the campus.

"You know what would be really cool?" Smitty said after Chelsea whisked past one day. "A school full of Chelsea Flynns."

SIX

Playing School

Name: Riana Tyson

Weighted GPA: 93.4—41st in the class of 109

SAT: 550 critical reading + 530 math = 1080 composite

ACT: 28

In Riana Tyson's background, college was almost a foreign concept. Her mother never attended one and neither did her brother or stepdad. As for her biological father, he was seldom part of her life. Only her stepbrother had gone. Now Riana was trying to be the second.

She knew one way was to play the standard high school game, perched in the front row, raising her hand, currying favor with teachers. But that wasn't her nature. In English class, which Riana found dull, she sat in the back and daydreamed. In history, they made her study notable figures she couldn't relate to. Science, however, was different. To her, physics was like doing puzzles about the universe, and chemistry explained how things worked in a way that got her thinking.

Riana was one of few African Americans at Oyster Bay High. She didn't open up with most adults at school, but she did trust Mr. Brown, the school's social worker. His office had a big leather couch and a guitar that a graduate had donated, and kids went there to talk.

"I've always been passionate about learning, just not about high school," she explained to Mr. Brown. It was too rigid, she told him. "They tell you what you have to do, what you have to think. Everything is set out for you, nothing is what you like. I don't play the game."

It's not that she was rebellious; she just preferred studying on her own terms. Riana did her most productive learning at the public library, an old stone building across the street from the high school. She was particularly intrigued by books on the solar system. She looked forward to each new issue of *Astronomy,* so she could check out her favorite feature, "The Stars This Month." In *Scientific American,* she liked to read about black holes and dark energy.

At night, she would wonder about the sky and later track down the answers. She wanted to know if other planets had life, and if so, was it possible those species pondered the same questions she did?

Riana's mother, growing up in Brooklyn, had dreamed of attending college to study fashion design, but life got in the way. She became pregnant with Riana's brother and was soon a single parent with bills to pay. To make ends meet, she had shared an apartment with a female friend. She tried to raise her kids to appreciate what they had. Once, when Riana's brother complained that other kids had more toys, his mom took him to the train station and pointed to a homeless woman living in a box. "That's all she has. She has no one to care for her, to hug, to talk to. I don't want to hear you complain again."

Riana was close to her mother, and even as a little girl, she was always sharing her latest life's plan with her: "Mom, I want to be an artist . . . an astronomer . . . open a restaurant . . . make a lot of money." No one in the family doubted that Riana was going to college.

In fourth grade, she started to notice that she was unlike her classmates at Theodore Roosevelt Elementary. Most were white; she was black. They lived in houses with pools or big yards; she lived in an apartment downtown. Many had money for ski trips and Caribbean vacations; she didn't. Seeing their easy lives made her resolve to someday make money of her own.

At the end of her sophomore year, a man with a ruddy face and a gray beard approached her in the hallway. "You did quite well on the practice PSAT, Riana Tyson."

Riana was flattered. Mr. Smith was keeping track of her?

She knew a little about the head of guidance: A lot of kids wanted him as their counselor senior year. She soon gained a better appreciation for him. The school library kept sending her bills for a book she was sure she'd returned. She went to see if Mr. Smith could help. She showed him the bill and explained the problem.

"I'll take care of it," he said, and ripped the notice in half.

Mr. Smith asked her to sign up for an evening course that met a dozen times during junior year to prepare kids for the PSATs. The course was free, except for a sixty-dollar materials fee. She agreed to sign up, and then seemingly forgot about it. When he reminded her, she let it drop again. Finally, Mr. Smith called Riana's mother. "I don't want to get personal, but is the cost of the program the reason she's not signing up?"

As she started to hedge, he interrupted. "I have extra materials," he said. "Everything she needs. I want her in this program. She has a future that can be very bright."

Riana's mom said she appreciated Smitty's interest. She had a job coordinating shipping for a printing company and worked long hours; she could do only so much to prepare her daughter for college.

Riana went to the prep course a couple of times, but learning test-taking strategies seemed a lot like playing the school game. She took the SAT once, without studying. She was more interested in real challenges. She'd known a few people with drinking and drug problems, so she joined Students Against Destructive Decisions. She helped organize Red Ribbon Week to warn kids about substance abuse. SADD met every Tuesday night, and it was followed by Undecided, the informal counseling group. During her junior year, she was elected president of both.

Riana developed a group of friends from all over, like Kasper, whose parents were from Iran, and Zara, whose parents were from Bangladesh. Junior year, her lab partner in physics was a cross-country runner named Andreas whose family was from Greece. He wasn't into playing the school game either. He was quiet in class, but, like her, was bright and into reading science books on the side. He wanted to be an engineer. He talked about string theory and supersymmetry; she talked about parallel universes and gravitational waves. Andreas was friendly enough, but he seemed to have a protective layer around himself. Riana thought something must have happened to make him so wary. A few times, she invited him to drop by the SADD meetings. He said he'd think about it, but he didn't show up.

As Riana finished junior year, her mother and stepfather bought a small house in another school district. It meant Riana could spend her senior year at a big high school with more science courses and a large African American population. But she didn't want to transfer.

Riana's mother wrote a letter to the school board saying her daughter had benefited from Oyster Bay's academics and wanted permission to attend from out of the district so that she could finish where she started. The board said yes.

Soon after, Riana got a letter saying Mr. Smith would be her counselor. She had a good feeling about her last year of high school.

J ust as some of his kids resisted too much structure in class, Gwyeth Smith Jr. had never liked playing the high school administrative game. For example, New York State asked tenth graders to do an "interest inventory" with a counselor. Smitty saw it as a forced process. Interest inventory? He wanted to connect with students naturally, not by filling out a form no one would read.

"When counselors have a genuine conversation with a youngster, they get to know his interests," he liked to say. "Isn't *that* an interest inventory?"

It wasn't the only area where he resisted bureaucratic rules.

A school where Smitty once worked required that counselors keep "accountability logs" to explain how they spent their time. Smitty refused. Were counselors supposed to write down when they went to the bathroom?

Nobody accused Smitty of sloughing off the job. He liked to say that his son and daughter had grown up and moved away, so he had no dependents other than five abandoned black cats that he and Kathi had taken in. That left him with a lot of flexibility, and he made good use of it. He worked right through the summer, he announced football games in the fall, ran the shot clock at basketball games and the timer at wrestling matches in the winter, and officiated track meets in the spring. He proctored exams on Saturdays, and stayed many evenings to accommodate the schedules of working parents. The district paid him $150,000. Smitty wasn't into high living, but as one of his few indulgences, he did enjoy driving a leased Lexus.

Phyllis Harrington, Oyster Bay's superintendent, tolerated Smitty's disdain for "administrivia," as she called it. "If I had to weigh the importance of getting a piece of paper in time or having the real work that Gwyeth does so masterfully, I realize it's okay that I'm not going to get the paper."

Smitty appreciated the trust, but it didn't stop him from challenging the superintendent at times. She'd spent her career in elementary education, and he often told her that administrators needed to focus their energy on the high school. "People don't move to a district because of the quality of the elementary school," Smitty said. "They move because of the quality of the high school." Home buyers often judge a district by the percentage of kids going on to top colleges.

It probably wasn't smart politics to challenge top brass, but Smitty felt he had to stand up for his constituency. "The way Smitty looks at it," explained Matt Brown, the social worker, "he's accountable first to the kids, second to the parents, and third to the district."

A few years earlier, a senior had wanted to take an advanced chemistry course that wasn't offered at Oyster Bay because a teacher had retired unexpectedly. So Smitty found an afternoon class at Long Island University's C.W. Post Campus, a few miles away. Smitty knew it would be a hassle to arrange official transportation through the school district, so he did it his own way. He arranged for a taxi company to bring the kid back and forth, and had the school district pay. The boy got into Yale.

Smitty even took on the teachers' union. He felt unions had done important work in the past, but had gradually become an obstacle to improving schools. Oyster Bay High's principal told of a morning when Smitty sent a memo to teachers requesting that eleventh-grade math and English devote class time to preparing kids for the PSAT. The new union representative went to the guidance office to complain.

Less than a minute later, he emerged, looking chastened.

"Let me guess," the principal said sympathetically. "Gwyeth told you to get the f___out."

The union rep nodded.

Toward the end of September, Smitty asked Riana to come to his office. He was concerned about her. She'd been very quiet since school started. He knew she was carrying a big course load. Smitty had helped her schedule seven straight classes—no free periods in between— so she could leave school early to do her library exploring. After a few hours there, he knew, she walked a mile to her job at a drugstore, where she worked from four till ten P.M.

Smitty leaned toward Riana. "Go ahead, talk to me."

Riana said it was hard commuting from a different district. Her mother couldn't pick her up in the afternoons, so they didn't have dinner together. She didn't get along with her stepfather.

Smitty asked about the college search.

Riana said she wanted to study chemical engineering and find a good job. She was looking at a variety of schools, starting with Cornell, Syracuse, and Buffalo.

"Could I ask how you like snowy places, and cold places?"

"I hate the cold. I can't lie but—"

"Have you looked at a weather report for Buffalo?"

"Yeah, but I'm willing to sacrifice. I like what I hear about the school."

"Then there's some give and take in where you go."

Smitty moved on to a set of questions he liked to put in front of students.

"I want to ask about four things that may sound silly: weather, distance, size, and setting. Which one would be the most important factor in finding your 'wow' school?"

"Setting."

"The setting should be large? Small? In a city? Or just a campus?"

"Medium to large. I would like to be close to a city."

"How about way out there in the countryside?"

"No *way*!"

He chuckled at her sudden fervor.

"I love this girl," Smitty said mostly to himself. He decided to challenge her.

"Okay, I'm going to suggest you look at some other places; some pretty competitive schools. I want you to take a look at the Web site of James Madison University. Great place, my son went there. It's part of the University of Virginia system. Also, I don't think you're going to like this because you're more of a name-brand person—but look into University of Mary Washington. It's also in the Virginia system."

She wrote that down.

"I would love to give you SUNY Geneseo—gorgeous place—but it's upstate and it's cold."

Smitty advised Riana to sign up for a diversity weekend at Cornell. It would be a convenient way to explore whether that school was a fit.

Then Smitty remembered another campus he liked. "I want you to do something with the College of New Jersey. Used to be Trenton State. A fairly competitive place. It's the Geneseo of New Jersey, by Princeton, with a beautiful lake on campus. It is equidistant between New York City and Philadelphia, so you've got access to two cities, two cultural centers."

Riana frowned.

He tried to tease out the problem. "Is it because of the size? Or the—"

"Because it's in New Jersey."

It was a common New York attitude. Smitty laughed at her stubbornness. "You're a very special girl, I will tell you that."

"Thank you, you're very special, too," she said playfully.

As Smitty stood up to walk Riana out, something occurred to him. "I forgot to ask. Your mother picks you up when?"

"When I'm done working at ten."

Smitty whistled at her crowded schedule—school, library, work, clubs, and any day now she'd start doing applications as well. He worried that sooner or later, something would have to give.

SEVEN

The Admissions
Industrial Complex

S mitty walked down the corridor of a Marriott hotel in Austin, Texas,
wearing plaid shorts and a polo shirt. He was on a mission for Allyson
Frankel. It was near the end of September, the final day of the annual
conference of the National Association for College Admission Counseling. Smitty had been attending for a quarter century, since the time only
a few hundred met in small venues. This year's conference was at Austin's
enormous convention center and every hotel within a mile was sold out. A
digital sign flashed "5,259," announcing the record number of counselors,
admissions officers, and other attendees.

One of those was Emory University's dean of admissions.

Many parents, Smitty said, could do parts of his job—push their kids
toward challenging courses, search for colleges that might suit them, and
insist they revise application essays. Yet this was something hard to replicate: building a network of contacts in admissions offices.

Smitty felt the thousand dollars or so he spent going to this conference each year was an investment for Oyster Bay kids. It helped offer a public school like his the same access as wealthy districts and private academies.

Smitty had known Emory's previous admissions dean, but he'd recently been promoted to another job. When Smitty saw the chance to grab the new dean for a moment, he approached her. He told her Emory had become popular at Oyster Bay, then he made his point. "We've got this wonderful girl—very good grades, involved in the community," Smitty said. "Older sister is a senior at Emory, last name is Frankel."

The dean smiled. Smitty was well regarded enough for his pitches to be taken seriously.

"Let me give you my direct line," she offered.

"But," Smitty continued, "her scores aren't as high as we'd like: 1270 on the SAT, 29 on the ACT."

Her smile faded. "I would say that it is going to be tough to not be in the mid-1300s from your area," she said.

Smitty got the message—Allyson should steer away from Emory. He chatted with the dean for a minute more, and then stepped aside as other guidance counselors approached with their own pitches. As Smitty moved on, he had one thought for Allyson: *Michigan.*

He hoped she was coming to the same conclusion.

Smitty always found it helpful to connect personally with those in admissions offices. He noticed the differences among them. There were three types. First, there were the newcomers just out of college themselves, often dabbling while they saved money for grad school. They were idealistic and liked a kid with a good story. The second type, the careerists, remained rooted in one school and one town. The third were those who sought to move up the ladder, college to college, sometimes rising to director or dean. To Smitty, it was especially helpful to keep in contact with those folks since their influence could grow over time.

Mary Beth Carey was an example. Smitty had gotten to know her twenty years before at an admissions training conference, and followed her as she moved from Marist College to the College of Saint Elizabeth to Saint Peter's College to Hofstra, and then to Drew University in New Jersey, which had become popular with Oyster Bay kids.

This year, it seemed like a strong option for one of the school's seniors who had a combined 1000 on the two key parts of the SATs, a mediocre number. The girl's mother was hoping to send her to Cornell. Smitty knew that would be impossible. But Drew was now test optional.

When Smitty spotted Mary Beth, he asked about her dog by name: "How's Bayley?" They caught up and Smitty made his pitch: "Got a young-ster for you. Good with computers. Doesn't test well."

"Send her my way," Mary Beth responded. "I'll make sure we give her a good look."

The National Association for College Admission Counseling held its first national conference in 1947 with forty-seven people. Now it filled a two-block-long convention center, and ran hundreds of seminars on everything from admissions trends to counseling gay and transgender teens. Attendees could meet vendors selling test prep and other services. But for many like Smitty, the real purpose was three days of mingling with hundreds of admissions officers.

He hoped such chats would lead to a match for up-in-the-air students like Chelsea Flynn and Riana Tyson. And he had other Oyster Bay kids to place, including several with learning disabilities. Of course, he could have picked possible schools for them while sitting at his computer, but the conference let him suss out which schools were interested and how their financial aid budgets looked.

Before he left, Smitty needed some face time with Fordham's vice president for undergraduate enrollment to get a sense of Jeff Sanders's chances.

Of the 1,540 colleges and universities that belong to the National Association for College Admission Counseling, the overall acceptance rate was 71 percent. Smitty found that reassuring, but he knew that parents of top-performing students care mostly about the handful of schools with rates of less than 20 percent. As he roved through the three-story conference center, he spotted a man in a red bow tie. It was William Shain, who had recently become admissions dean at Bowdoin College. Smitty made it his job to know the background of people like Shain: He'd gone to Princeton and Columbia Law, taught at a high school, then worked in admissions at Princeton, Macalester, and Vanderbilt. He was part of the admissions industrial complex, but he also shared Smitty's skeptical view of it.

Smitty liked connecting with Bowdoin; as a teen living a few blocks from campus, he'd sneaked into basketball games at halftime to watch a varsity captain named William Cohen, who later became a U.S. senator and then secretary of defense.

Smitty asked Shain how he liked the new job.

"I haven't made peace with the rejection rate," Shain said. "We're turning away more than eighty percent of applicants."

"Eighty percent!" Smitty whistled.

Shain agreed the number was up there and he assumed it would get tougher. Boards of trustees and alumni wanted their schools to be seen as increasingly sought after. Admissions deans were competitive, too.

Smitty knew it's no fun to travel the country trying to lure more and more applicants, only to have to turn down most of them. Admissions directors at such schools particularly dread calls from alumni whose kids didn't make it.

But Smitty pointed out the upside—at least for Bowdoin. "Makes the families even more eager to get into a school," he said. "They do want that window decal."

Shain agreed, yet he felt a rejection from any single school shouldn't matter so much because there were so many great alternatives out there. He gestured to the conference hall, where hundreds of colleges had set up booths.

"I want to say, stop worrying about your son or daughter being rejected," Shain told Smitty. "They'll get an education, they'll have friends, they'll get jobs." Shain used himself as an example. He went to Princeton, but looking back, it was an intimidating place, and he might have been happier at a smaller school.

The conference tried to address that issue with a seminar called "Swimming with the Sharks." The speaker, from a high-pressure New Jersey school district, spoke of how parents care more about prestige than the right fit.

"Get over yourself," the speaker said. "Don't worry about the bumper sticker on the back of your Volvo."

Another seminar was given by a rep from the Stanford University School of Education's Stressed-Out Students Project. She talked about the emphasis on grades instead of learning, and asked a question: "Is the pressure to get into college turning high schools into morally bankrupt academic boot camps?"

She answered her own question with a yes.

Smitty had traveled to Austin with a Long Island friend who was in the college consulting business. He charged five hundred dollars per ninety-minute session to advise students. Each year, he and Smitty would rib each other about who was doing better in placing kids. Together this week, they'd flown in early to visit the University of Houston, Baylor, and Southern Methodist University. At Rice, they got a tour with Brady, a young man who'd graduated three months earlier from Oyster Bay. With Smitty's encouragement, he had turned down Cornell and five other universities to study engineering at Rice. As he showed Smitty around the pristine campus on the outskirts of downtown Houston, Brady told Smitty it was the right decision.

The two counselors then drove to the University of Texas at Austin, the friend reading aloud from his notes, almost as if cramming for a test. "UT, known as the Public Ivy . . . largest endowment for a public U., comes from the Santa Rita oil well in the Permian Basin . . . majors from botany to zoology . . . student population from egghead to Bible beater."

On campus, they met kids from New York who said they loved UT. Smitty added it to his list of recommended rah-rah schools.

I n the past few years, the conference had focused on the gender performance gap in high schools. Increasingly, girls had higher grades and graduation rates than boys. This time, one of the most crowded seminars was called "Where Would Holden Caulfield Get In?" The program explained that it was about underachieving boys.

Smitty had noticed girls surpassing boys academically for years. This season, of the ten Oyster Bay kids with the highest GPAs, only three were boys. To Smitty, the seminar could have been a case study of Jeff Sanders.

Jeff was in Smitty's thoughts one evening of the conference as he strolled through the New York delegation's cocktail party. In a corner by the cheese table, he found a man with owlish glasses, Fordham's vice president for undergraduate enrollment.

Smitty approached, made small talk, and then summarized Jeff: "Fantastic kid, great attitude, three varsity sports. He's met with your assistant basketball coach . . ."

"Sounds interesting."

Smitty wanted to show that Jeff had overcome challenges. "All kinds of relatives are living in this youngster's house," said Smitty. "There must be twenty dependents."

The man nodded.

"The boards are good," Smitty said, "but the grades from junior year weren't there. We've got him taking a much more ambitious schedule this year."

Behind his glasses, the Fordham dean looked intrigued. "I think he's going to be a stretch, but I'd like to see his preliminary transcript. He might be the kind of kid who makes the most of senior year."

It was probably the best response Smitty could hope for. He would be coming back to school with a warning. Jeff had a chance at Fordham, his first choice, but only if he stepped up.

EIGHT

"Is Donating Blood an Extracurricular?"

When he returned from the admissions conference, Smitty came into Essay Writing to sit with Allyson. "Still love Michigan?"

"I do," Allyson replied. To Smitty's relief, she was feeling more excited about it than Emory. She had even begun Michigan's application. Today was Monday, and she planned to send it out on Friday. "This week is my self-inflicted goal," she said, as kids nearby laughed. Kathi Reilly, who had overheard, said Allyson meant "self-imposed."

Smitty urged her to finish quickly since top students around the country saw Michigan as the "safe Ivy." They'd be applying by the thousands. Because Michigan had rolling admissions, students would hear fairly quickly but it wasn't binding. So Allyson could sit with a potential acceptance until spring and still change her mind.

Smitty liked youngsters to have an early yes. It had more to do with mental health than with strategy. Once a kid gets in somewhere, the family can relax a bit.

Smitty didn't tell Allyson that he'd gotten a lukewarm response from Emory's dean of admissions. He felt she could still try for it, perhaps in Emory's second early decision round. For most schools, the first ED deadline is mid-November, with a mid-December decision. Emory was among schools that offered a second ED deadline on January 1, with decisions a month later. That pool would still give Allyson slightly better odds than regular admission, and it would allow some time to receive Michigan's answer. Smitty knew it sounded complicated, but these were routine considerations for those playing the game.

E very October, Smitty found himself repeating three words to students: "Less is more." It applied to many parts of the college hunt. Less fancy writing in your essay. Less than ten schools on your list. Less thinking that there's only one perfect college for you. Less stress, period.

For the first couple of weeks of school, Smitty had let the kids find their own way, exploring colleges and essay topics. But when he got back from Texas on the first day of October, it was time for the guidance counselor to guide. One way he did that was to try selling more distant colleges. He told engineering students about Rice, and how his host, Brady, an Oyster Bay grad, was already feeling at home there. He mentioned Southern Methodist University—and don't be fooled by the name, Smitty remarked. "The president of the student body is Jewish."

He wasn't getting takers. The kids acted as if he were describing an alien world. Still he kept pushing. He'd met undergrads from New York who loved the University of Texas at Austin—with its nineteen libraries, including the LBJ library, containing forty-four million documents.

Finally, one of the boys showed some curiosity about Texas. "Mr. Smith," he asked, "how was the Mexican food?"

Smitty smiled and said he didn't like Mexican food. It was, though, a reminder that teenagers have their own priorities.

He moved on to deadlines. He reminded the kids that anyone applying early had just one month to finish everything. And before they knew it, December would arrive, and everyone would have to hustle. He said he hoped that at the least, they had begun their résumés—their list of extracurricular activities. Every class had its joker, and one mentioned that he'd heard about an upcoming blood drive. "Is donating blood an extracurricular?" he asked.

S mitty approached Jeff at his computer and said they needed to talk for a minute.

"I had a conversation with a vice president from Fordham," Smitty said.

Jeff looked up from his screen, which happened to be on ESPN's site. He said he hadn't given up on trying early for Fordham.

Smitty told him it wouldn't work. "You're simply not ready," he said. And not just for Fordham, but for any college. "They'll be forced to judge you by your grades from junior year, and that will be disastrous."

Smitty assured Jeff that he hadn't lost confidence in him. "You understand I believe you'll be a much stronger candidate in a couple of months?"

Jeff nodded. Smitty sensed that on some level he seemed relieved not to have to do his application in the next month.

S mitty had been pitching kids to admissions offices for three decades before having a chance to see what it was like from the receiving end. A few summers before, he'd been invited to a five-day workshop known as "admissions boot camp" that matched fifty guidance counselors with admissions deans from Harvard, Yale, Penn, Duke, Emory, Northwestern, and Michigan.

The counselors split into teams that received the actual files of eight kids who had applied to Yale, their names changed for privacy. The teams could admit only three candidates, and no one could be wait-listed. Smitty's team, led by Yale's dean, combed over eight sets of scores, essays, and recommendations, debating who should have an edge:

The salutatorian from Harlem with sagging test scores who had seen a man shot dead in a gang killing?

The Taiwanese American boy who had perfect scores on all his SAT and AP tests?

The mixed-race boy from a remote part of Oregon that had never sent a student to Yale?

The white girl from an Iowa college town who astonished an alum interviewer with her knowledge of literature, and then spoke to him in fluent French?

The white valedictorian from Ohio who had taken college classes in organic chemistry and advanced calculus?

The star student, also white, who started a middle-school mentoring project and never told her guidance counselor that she volunteered with Native Americans and the elderly?

The white boy from the Midwest who mastered Japanese but whose teacher said he needed to learn some humility?

Or finally:

The Korean girl from San Francisco—daughter of a taxi driver and a textile worker—who spoke English as a second language, yet became a debate champion?

Smitty, jotting observations on a yellow pad, noted that the salutatorian in Harlem was a Mexican American from a family with an income under twenty-five thousand dollars a year. His parents had never gone to college. Smitty voted to admit the boy.

The Taiwanese American, who spoke Chinese at home, impressed Smitty because he wasn't a stereotypical nerd. Smitty was charmed by his essay about working as a camp counselor and playing with sixth graders— even caring for them after some got sick and threw up. "Slam dunk," Smitty wrote. Admit.

He also admitted the student who started a mentoring project. He liked selfless leadership.

That was three. Smitty reluctantly passed on the others.

The process opened his eyes to some things. Admissions officers at the most selective schools see so many students with exceptional scores, they get numbed by the numbers. Parents and guidance counselors forget how many superstars are out there. "We become myopic," Smitty admitted. "We think our youngster is the finest ever." Really, he said, with such intense competition at the top, "It's a crapshoot."

Smitty also saw that admissions officers are impressed by unexpected details. His team admired the Taiwanese American boy's string of perfect scores, of course, but they spent more time discussing his essay on the joys of playing hide-and-seek as a camp counselor. "It was tender and sweet and fun," Smitty recalled. "It humanized him."

Only when the exercise was over did Yale's admissions dean reveal that all eight of the applicants had been accepted a few years earlier. In the end, Smitty decided the boot camp didn't change how he did his job; it reinforced the things he felt kids should emphasize.

Later, he shared five of them:

- A résumé should include only activities that a student is devoted to. Colleges don't want a big laundry list. "They won't read it," he said. "Or if they do, they won't believe it."

- At least one recommendation letter should come from the teacher of a core academic course taken in eleventh grade or after. It's also helpful to get letters from a scoutmaster or boss who truly knows the applicant. Letters from a member of Congress or the chairman of a company rarely impress the committee.
- Essays must be written by the student. Admissions officers have a surprising ability to see through those penned by parents or outsiders. "If someone with 550 verbal SAT scores produces a 750-level essay," Smitty said, "the reader begins to wonder about its legitimacy."
- Parents should fill out a "brag sheet" to help a guidance counselor fully appreciate a student before writing a recommendation. Bragging is not the same as exaggerating.
- A student who has overcome a hardship like a death in the family or a physical disability shouldn't feel compelled to write about it. A counselor's recommendation can take care of that.

Behind most of those rules lay Smitty's universal rule: Less is more.

Smitty had been asking Lee to cut his three-page résumé, but instead it had grown to seven pages, with activities set off by subtitles and bullets. Lee included his position as historian of the student council and his membership on his tenth-grade Catholic school wrestling team.

Smitty held up the résumé, clearly displeased.

"That's not a finished product," Lee offered weakly.

"I understand it's not finished," said Smitty, "but it can't be seven pages long. It's got to have some kind of flow." As a model, Smitty handed Lee a one-page résumé a student had done the previous year.

"You'll have to give me something clear so I can write your recommendation. Right now, my friend, it might as well be in Korean."

Smitty felt that seventeen-year-olds should keep a résumé to one page, two at the most. This year, several kids turned in long ones with fancy typefaces and jargon words like *impacted,* which suggested a parent's involvement. Colin, the crew recruit, showed up with a résumé that had a color photo of him rowing. It was too slick for Smitty, but he didn't say anything. The boy's talents had attracted the interest of coaches at Yale, Princeton, and Dartmouth, and he didn't need much help. That was another key to the college chase—the coach factor. Coaches understand that if they're to get a recruit through admissions, they have to assess not just sports skills but grades as well. Smitty knew that if a coach continued to show strong interest, a student was likely well on the way.

By now, Lee had decided to apply to Oxford. His application was due in two weeks. Smitty told him to go home and begin cutting his résumé.

Later, Matt Brown stopped by to chat. Smitty mentioned his frustration with Lee Kim. The boy was looking at some of the country's most competitive colleges, yet he didn't seem to want advice.

Matt said that Lee fooled people with his cool exterior. He was a deeper thinker than most folks suspected. He'd do well at a competitive college, where he could challenge his professors and classmates.

"He's a sleeper," Matt said.

Smitty looked at him, waiting for more.

Matt explained that Lee was working out all kinds of conflicts about his place in his family, in the Korean immigrant community, and in the Catholic Church. But Lee was unlikely to tell Smitty any of that.

Like Smitty, Kathi wanted to teach lessons that would stick long after students clicked the SUBMIT button on their applications. One was her own "less is more" lesson. She believed that, from the time they were in elementary school, students were praised whenever they wrote extra long school papers. Schools failed to teach the value of disciplined writing. As the kids began their application essays, Kathi emphasized concise prose. She stapled another maxim to a bulletin board: "Use the active voice instead of the passive voice. State who did what, not what was done by whom."

Kathi went over seven other rules:

- Hook the reader with the opening.
- Focus on a small subject, or a moment, even if you want to convey a big idea.
- Prune unneeded adjectives and adverbs—and that means most of them.
- Avoid "ten-dollar SAT words."
- Show, don't tell.
- Have an ending that leaves the reader wanting more.
- Read every essay aloud to make sure it sounds right—even if your family thinks you sound crazy.

A couple of days before Allyson's self-inflicted deadline, she handed Kathi her essay. It was on Michigan's question about why she chose her academic area of interest. Allyson had been picturing the thousands of applications landing in Michigan's admissions building. She wanted to write something that stood out from the other essays.

She began with an unusual image: a young woman performing before a mirror while being observed by a panel of judges. At first, Kathi wasn't clear where Allyson was going. But as she read on, she realized it was a device for Allyson to describe what it felt like to be a college applicant. She was able to look in the mirror and see all her own talents, but would the judges be able to?

"How could she convey the reflection she knew so well to the audience who knew so little about her?" Allyson wrote. "How could she capture the essence of herself just by answering one question about her interests?"

A few lines later, Allyson added some descriptions of herself:

She's conceptual, a real free thinker. She thrives on other people's energy, and is profoundly sensitive to their emotions. She loves neon colors, splattered paint, and clay between her fingers. . . . She has a desire to help others heal through art therapy, and if the panel approved her performance she would show them all of this, not just tell them.

Kathi liked it. It was truly a writer's essay. She did notice some inconsistent tenses and some words that could be changed. She and Smitty knew that ethically they shouldn't overedit a student's essay. But it was fine to suggest revisions and talk about rules of good writing. And it would make kids better writers in college.

Allyson's essay was almost ready to go. *Show, don't tell,* Kathi said every day, and Allyson had done just that. "Beautiful," Kathi wrote in the margin in red pen.

Smitty and Kathi rented a carriage house at the edge of an old estate that was home to a wild turkey and four llamas. In the evenings, Kathi sat on a leather couch in the den reading essays while Smitty relaxed on a matching couch poring over the sports section of the paper. Their five black cats prowled around them.

That night, Kathi passed Allyson's essay to Smitty. He felt it would impress any admissions officer. Allyson shouldn't order a Michigan Wolverine sweatshirt just yet, but if she met her deadline, she'd take a big step closer to Ann Arbor.

NINE

Regular Kids from the Suburbs

By the time seniors started applying to colleges, they realized something unsettling: It was too late to improve most factors that admissions offices would evaluate. Grade point averages had been calculated. There was no more time to land an impressive internship or become president of a club. Many of the kids were already done with the SAT and ACT.

Smitty had good news, though. One thing was still in the students' control: the essay. "This is completely in your hands," he told them. "It's your story to tell."

For many applicants, the essay was an afterthought, hurriedly composed and revised. At Oyster Bay, though, Smitty's kids had a semester-long class to perfect theirs—forty-two minutes a day, five days a week, till the last deadline in mid-January.

Smitty liked to listen to Kathi critiquing kids' writing. She'd never had kids of her own, and she treated Oyster Bay's students like surrogate children. Often the essays stirred up strong feelings in their writers. Having lost her own father to cancer when she was thirteen, Kathi could empathize as kids struggled on paper with personal issues.

At first, many of the students insisted they didn't like to write—and had nothing to say. Kathi would question them about their travels or their families. "That's it!" she'd say when someone told a compelling anecdote. "Now put it into paragraphs."

Admissions reps told Smitty they looked forward to reading essays from Oyster Bay High. The kids' writing had gotten attention elsewhere, too. Several years earlier, a book called *Writing an Outstanding College Application Essay* had included nineteen examples from Oyster Bay, more than any other school. There was something even more rewarding to Smitty and Kathi: When Oyster Bay kids went to college, many reported back that the training in room 207 prepared them to handle professors' assignments.

Every so often, nearby districts sent teachers and counselors to observe Essay Writing for College. Many left wanting to replicate the class, but they didn't get the backing of their schools. Smitty thought that was a shame. He'd seen a nationwide survey by the National Association for College Admission Counseling that found admissions offices rank essays fifth in importance—after grades in college prep courses, standardized tests, GPA, and rank. Most recently, 23 percent of colleges reported that an applicant's essay has "considerable importance" in the admissions decision, compared to 14 percent in the 1990s. Smitty's instincts told him the impact was far greater. He had often found that a great essay could sway admissions officers into accepting a borderline applicant, and even a long shot.

Because most kids never have an admissions interview, Smitty saw the essay as the one chance for a student's voice to be heard. Far more than a transcript, it conveyed who they were.

"I want the admissions person to close his eyes and envision you,"

Smitty told Jeff's first-period class. "Let's face it: You probably will never get closer to them than you do in the essay."

It was a message he especially wanted Jeff to hear. Jeff had shown up late to first period in room 207 several times, not a good sign in October, the start of the early admissions homestretch. But today Smitty wouldn't be able to scold Jeff for being late. He had skipped class altogether.

Good writing hooked the reader, Kathi told the students. It intrigued; it surprised; sometimes it shocked. But a college essay could do that only if it avoided humdrum formulas.

Too many, she said, began with a banal "I" sentence: "I walked onto the campus of XYZ University and felt I had found my place." One such "I" sentence led to another, Kathi warned: "I developed an interest in chemistry in eleventh grade." First person can work fine if it's a compelling anecdote, she continued, or if it has a strong voice, but if not, all those sentences sounded self-centered.

As models, Kathi chose several of her favorite essays by past students. When she read them aloud in a soothing voice, the kids said they were reminded of bedtime stories.

"'My college search was overwhelming, terrifying, and the leading cause of death for countless pencils.'" (That one went on to tell why the student liked Penn's biomed program.)

"'Band geek. This title has followed me since the fourth grade.'" (By a girl who had found herself through music.)

"'Once upon a time, I lived on Easy Street.'" (By a girl who watched her father go to jail.)

"'The more friends you have, the better off you are. This was the advice my dad gave me when I was ten.'" (By a girl whose father was killed during a robbery at his store in New York City)

"'I'm a political junkie. I feel like I've let myself down if I haven't voted for homecoming king and queen. Most of my friends hang pictures of pop stars in their lockers. I hang pictures of presidents.'" (By a boy who wanted to study politics in Washington, D.C.)

"'I value uniqueness. I value nakedness.'" (By a girl responding to an essay about her personality.)

"Nakedness?!" A couple of the boys cracked up at that. Kathi pointed out that it got their attention, a sign of good writing. She was willing to bet that the boys would read more of that essay, and so would a bleary-eyed admissions officer.

After studying what others had written in past years, the kids tried hooking readers with their own opening sentences.

"Pure silence never sounds this loud." (A girl, describing her favorite activity, running.)

"Where was that owl?" (Adati, daughter of Indian immigrants, relating her efforts to find a hidden part of a statue while walking around Columbia.)

"I stared at the man with the bright yellow sunglasses, focusing on his smile." (That was Zara, a daughter of immigrants from Bangladesh, relating the day she took photos of a chess player in a park.)

"My friends drive new cars. I drive a beat-up '97 Honda Civic. They shop at Abercrombie. I shop at Marshalls. And growing up they were always bigger and taller and faster and stronger." (Another girl, recounting how she found a way to fit in by playing basketball.)

Kathi assured the kids the first paragraph was often the toughest. Within a few days, most were finishing their initial drafts, and sitting in small groups to compare their different approaches. They seemed to have forgotten that they didn't like writing.

. . .

A few weeks after starting work at Oyster Bay in 1999, Smitty had chaperoned a group of kids taking a bus trip to a soccer playoff. Once on the road, the boys began talking trash about girls and singing explicit rap lyrics. Smitty had the bus pull over so he could tell the kids to tone it down. When they reached the soccer field, two boys bolted out the back door and set off the alarm.

He felt it was a sign that Oyster Bay High had issues with rowdiness, and over the next few months he worked with fellow administrators to change the tenor.

These days, he thought, Oyster Bay seemed a different place. He gave some of the credit to his friend Matt Brown, who tried to get kids to examine their behavior. Once a year, Matt ran "Challenge Day," in which a group of facilitators from California spent eight hours in the gym helping kids talk to one another about everything from being bullied to being forgotten amid parents' divorces.

Riana had played a role in the changes, too. She was attracting forty or more kids to the weekly SADD meetings. They would stop goofing around as soon as she walked in and said, "May I have your attention?"

Smitty sensed the change even in his college class. On almost any day, he would see kids critiquing one another's essays—very different from the cut-throat atmosphere at schools where some students wouldn't even tell class-mates where they'd applied. In room 207, they cheered one another on.

One day Adati was stuck for a subject. "I'm supposed to write about something that's important to people our age," she told Kathi. But she was at a loss.

Kathi asked the class to chip in.

"Health care," someone called out from a computer.

"Boring!" Kasper exclaimed.

"Politics."

"Everybody writes about that."

Allyson, who knew that Adati traveled regularly to India, said, "Why don't you write about how frustrated you are that Americans aren't interested in the rest of the world?" That struck a chord. Kathi and Adati looked at each other and smiled.

"You have your subject," Kathi said.

Smitty told the seniors about a boy who had graduated from Oyster Bay three years earlier. He'd floundered in his first attempts at an essay. Then he came back with one that Smitty found chilling. It was about taking a flight back to New York from a tennis camp in Florida in early September 2001. The boy described sitting next to two sullen men who kept their heads buried in books. Hungry after a day of exercise, he asked for their cookies, which they wordlessly handed over. Only when FBI agents visited the boy's house a week later, did he realize he'd eaten the cookies of two of the terrorists who went on to hijack planes on 9/11.

Most kids, Smitty said, would have overdramatized the anecdote, but the boy handled it in a restrained manner that reflected his own measured character. He was admitted to Brown. Smitty told the class that an essay's tone—its voice—can say as much about an applicant's personality as the content.

Smitty could count on the students to pose a particular question every year as they brainstormed for an essay idea. "What if you don't have a tragedy in your family?" a boy said. "My father never went to jail."

Smitty said the essay doesn't have to be about something traumatic; it just has to reveal who you are. "Make yourself real," Smitty said. "Don't write what you believe others want to hear."

A few years before, one boy wrote a compelling composition on his almost embarrassingly normal life.

"I've lived an average and uneventful existence," his Stony Brook essay began. But he also used it to reveal his passion for writing, which he'd developed in eighth grade. That, said Smitty, is the winning combination—tell your truths and show your strengths.

Kathi agreed that kids tried too hard to wow an admissions office with some supposedly life-changing event. "Bigger isn't necessarily better," she warned. She went to the binders and pulled out a boy's Tufts essay. The school had asked applicants to write on the following topic: "Describe an environment in which you were raised."

While many reached for the most heightened interpretation, this boy found drama in something mundane but universal. He chose his kitchen.

In most suburban homes, the front door leads to a welcoming foyer. Step into our house, however, and you'll find yourself smack in the middle of the kitchen, facing three barking dogs, an obstacle course of backpacks, and the debris of my eight-year-old sister's latest artistic creation.

When we sit down to dinner, conversation turns to the events of the day, starting with school, then leading to local and world events. With three other siblings vying for commentary and parents with opposing political views, things can get animated. Often someone's comment triggers an argument, and while it can be maddening, it is never dull.

The boy addressed those who might question the value of an average upbringing:

In preparing for admissions, I've read a number of essays by students who seem almost embarrassed to be "regular kids" from the suburbs. We may seem provincial, but my home has created a sort of stable chaos, where I can witness disagreements, tolerance, negotiations, and acceptance. I think I've received some of my best education there in that kitchen.

Like many good essays, this one used what Kathi called three "uns": unusual details; unexpected twist; and understated tone. She particularly liked the oxymoron "stable chaos."

She told kids not to be afraid of enlivening an unexceptional moment by looking at it through fresh eyes. She gave the example of a student who worked at a hair salon, watched a homeless woman enter, and told the story from the viewpoint of a customer: "She was ugly standing inside a beauty parlor . . . an abstract idea that did not belong."

The key, Kathi kept saying, is to make it personal. She read aloud an essay by a girl who captured herself with a few brushstrokes:

I love cherry ChapStick. I bite my nails. I don't know if I believe in fate, but I do not believe in God.

I want to learn how to fly. I'd like to dance in the rain on a hot summer night, and leap into puddles that seem the size of oceans. I hope that someday I'll play the guitar. I find perfection in a new pack of crayons, in which every crayon is sharp, lustrous, and begging to be used.

Kathi had a hunch that this one would impress Chelsea. Sure enough, Chelsea was smiling as she listened. Kathi felt certain Chelsea would produce her own memorable essay—though likely on her own schedule.

Many guidance counselors told students to avoid controversial subjects, but Smitty disagreed. The admissions reps he knew liked boldness, and they wanted to attract a student body with all sorts of viewpoints.

"Put a stake in the ground," he told kids. "It's fine at seventeen to have a strong opinion." Years before, one of his students had written about being a skinhead, and was ultimately accepted at Bates College in Maine—not known for recruiting skinheads. Later, Smitty was glad to hear the boy's politics had changed.

An Oyster Bay boy wrote about volunteering at the Republican National Convention and becoming disillusioned with ideologues from all parties including his own. "I suddenly felt as if I no longer fit in with my counterparts," he wrote. "My views tend to be conservative, but that does not mean I will isolate myself, refusing to listen to the other side or treat them with any less respect."

The boy went on to study political science at his first-choice school, GWU.

Lee Kim wasn't yet ready to decide on an essay, although his thoughts often turned to weighty matters. He was having a crisis of faith.

At the Catholic boys' school he'd attended, he observed that kids succeeded by parroting information back to teachers. Lee wasn't like that. He'd challenged everyone, demanding to know why God allowed war and famine. At one point, after a wrestling practice in tenth grade, a couple of the boys punched and kicked Lee in the locker room. He complained to a faculty member, who did nothing. To Lee, it seemed more than a coincidence that the bullies were from influential families. When they picked on the son of a Korean funeral director, it didn't seem to matter. He wondered: Where was the school's Christian spirit?

While serving as an altar boy at Christmas Mass that year, he began to ponder such things. If Catholics were certain their religion was most benevolent, but Protestants and Muslims believed the same about their faiths, who was right? How could every religion be the one true faith?

How could religions that celebrated peace also justify the Crusades or ethnic cleansing?

Lee considered his parents model Christians. His father often refused to take payment for the funeral of a child. Yet his mom and dad occasionally went to a psychic, an action that went against Catholic doctrine.

He was starting to see faith as a crutch. "As humans," Lee would say, "we need someone to blame, someone to give us hope, so we have religions. Every society has some spiritual and mythical system because mankind needs an explanation for what we cannot rationally explain."

Lee's constant doubts prompted him to leave parochial school. As soon as he got back to Oyster Bay, he heard the rumors. "People say I stole things, or I got into fights with everyone and got expelled." He didn't care enough to deny it. He knew who he was.

His crisis about religion deepened during his junior year, when his ex-girlfriend was struck and killed by a phone company truck while crossing the street in New York City. He'd learned in Sunday school that death was part of God's ultimate plan. If that was the case, it was an inane plan.

"Why," he would ask, "would God have a truck hit a caring, bright girl? How can a religion possibly say this is the way her life should end?"

Lee's missionary trips had added to his doubts. He saw families scratching the dirt to plant crops while the people who were proselytizing assured them that belief in God was their salvation. What the people really needed was practical information about crop rotation and microcredit, Lee thought.

Sometimes he suspected that kids in places like Long Island believed their form of salvation meant getting into a prestigious university. Was that really a guarantee of money and happiness?

So while other kids obsessed about college, he grappled with larger questions. Did every society have a deity? What would people believe in if they didn't have religion?

Lee met with Mr. Smith from time to time, but didn't share these thoughts. Although Mr. Smith said colleges wanted honest application essays, Lee doubted the people in an admissions factory really cared about his personal struggles.

Smitty didn't like to meddle in kids' relationships, but he was glad to hear that Jeff Sanders's girlfriend had given herself a challenge. She'd decided to help Jeff work more efficiently on his apps. Jenna bought a colorful accordion folder and labeled a space for each college Jeff was considering. She helped him make a to-do list of the materials that each school required. When someone in the first-period class asked about his rainbow-colored folder, Jeff blushed. But he also looked pleased.

Jenna and Jeff had grown up on the same street, two houses apart. They'd been friends since fourth grade, and started dating junior year. Jeff appeared to be the stereotype of a jock, but Jenna found him to be much more.

She often saw his selfless side. While he didn't mind weekend partying, he was also devoted to his family. When they were in tenth grade, Jeff had stopped by her house one day, dribbling a basketball, as always. "My little cousins are moving in, so I'll be babysitting on Friday nights if you want to come by sometime," he said.

Senior year, Jeff had to share his bedroom with his four-year-old cousin. It was a lot to ask of a boy Jeff's age. Instead of complaining, he kept his focus on others, asking his friends about their own family problems.

Jenna's grade point average was thirty points higher than her boyfriend's, but in some ways, she observed, Jeff was more focused than she was. "He's always had a clear idea of what he wants to do," she said. While some saw him as sports obsessed, she felt he approached athletics as a vocation. He was constantly reading about college players and coaches, soaking up stats, and thinking about a sports management career.

Jenna's father had been a star quarterback in Oyster Bay, and in the 1970s he'd gone to Penn State on scholarship to play football for Joe Paterno. But after two years he'd returned home to work as a bayman. In some ways, Jeff served as the son he'd never had, and a quarterback, no less. The two spent hours talking sports, and Jeff's command of minutiae from decades earlier amazed Jenna's father.

Jenna was convinced that Jeff would achieve great things, and Smitty agreed. He saw Jeff as the kind of kid who floundered in high school classes but would thrive at college, where he could study what interested him.

First he had to get in, though. The challenge now was to get him energized about his applications and essay. With Jeff showing up late for Essay Writing for College, and sometimes not at all, Smitty wasn't sure when that would happen.

And then, one morning in the middle of October, Smitty walked into room 207 and found Jeff at a computer. This time, he wasn't looking at the ESPN or Sports Illustrated sites; he was at a keyboard writing intently about the day his car was stolen.

> I learned at a young age that when faced with a bad situation, it's best to find a positive. When my dog died, although I was upset I knew I wouldn't miss cleaning up my backyard. When my brother moved, I was saddened, but getting my own bedroom was a way to forget about the gloom. In all aspects of life, I try to find as many positives as I can.
>
> My philosophy was put to the test this past summer.

Jeff was stepping up to the job. Smitty patted him on the back and left him alone with his thoughts.

TEN

Parenting the Parents

E verything came crashing down for Riana one Tuesday morning.

As she walked into school, she made a mental list of the too many things she needed to do: calculus assignment, choose colleges, history test, write application essay, get to work, talk to Mr. Brown about SADD, find time for . . .

Suddenly she started crying. She turned a corner and almost ran into Mr. Smith in the hallway. It was clear to him that she needed to talk.

"You are not going to your class," he said. "Come to my office."

When she got there, she sat silently and looked at the ground.

"Am I supposed to guess what's going on, or are you going to tell me?" Mr. Smith asked.

She didn't answer.

"This has to do with home?"

"Yes."

"School?"

"Yes."

"Boyfriend?"

"No."

"Work?"

"Yes."

Smitty had long ago learned those were four standard issues for high school girls.

"Okay. Guessing game over. Take a breath, then fill me in."

She told him that with so much going on, she couldn't keep up with her schoolwork. She was arguing with her stepfather about everything, and about nothing.

"I am so overwhelmed, Mr. Smith. I am so far behind."

Smitty was quiet for a moment. He was known as a good listener; he let silences fall to make sure he didn't jump in too quickly. But Riana was done.

"You are on the run all day long," he said. "It's not a question of your ability. It's that Mom drops you off at seven-thirty in the morning and you're running till ten-thirty at night."

Riana sniffled.

"How vital is it for you to be working?"

She said she wanted the job. Other kids got cell phones and credit cards and cash from their parents, but she didn't. She liked to go out, too, sometimes. "I don't spend much, but it's nice to have some money in my pocket."

"And I understand that."

Riana had inquired at the drugstore about reducing her hours, but they couldn't accommodate such a part-time schedule.

"You need to learn to ask for help, my dear," Smitty said. "You're seventeen, you don't have to deal with it all yourself."

It was the middle of October, and her class assignments and college applications were going to become only more demanding. Smitty said he'd help her make a schedule of deadlines and talk to her about time management. As soon as Riana left, he called her mother.

When Smitty met with guidance counselors from other districts, he heard about parents who second-guessed every step of the application process. Some called them hummingbird, or hovercraft, parents.

A guidance director friend of Smitty's on Long Island told of asking a stressed-out student how many schools he'd applied to. The boy's response explained a lot of his stress. "Fourteen," the boy said. Then he added in a flat tone, "And my mother applied to eighteen."

As moms and dads became more invested in the process over the years, Smitty had noticed a shift in pronouns. "My son loves Northwestern and he is applying" became "We are applying." Smitty had heard of parents lobbying for kids by calling college admissions officers and even sending them chocolates or liquor. So far that hadn't happened in his district—at least he hadn't heard of it. As he put it, "The vast majority of our parents find the right balance. They're involved without being obsessed."

This year he felt especially lucky. Many of the seniors had backgrounds that gave parents perspective. Allyson and Chelsea had older siblings who had applied to competitive colleges, and their folks knew not to micromanage. As for Jeff, his parents were busy with a house full of relatives and relieved to sign over the college search to Smitty. Similarly, Riana's mother, with no college application experience herself, was glad to follow his lead.

But there were one or two who did obsess.

One afternoon, a mother called Smitty to say she had an urgent problem. She was whispering, and Smitty could barely hear her. She explained that she was in the garage. Her daughter was in the house crying because she was so stressed about her admissions essays. The mother mentioned a private college consultant who was working with her. As the mother talked, Smitty realized the girl was getting advice from four people: her Oyster Bay guidance counselor, her English teacher Kathi, a private educational adviser, and her mother. Smitty told the mom to use the guidance department or the private consultant to shape strategy, but not both.

One day, another mom asked to see Smitty. She said her son was applying to the University of North Carolina at Chapel Hill. It was a great place, she said, and her son's top choice. Smitty recalled that the boy had average grades and scores. UNC could have worked had he been a recruited athlete, star musician, or class president, but he wasn't. He was a nice kid, with no special hook. And he was a New Yorker trying to get into a school with limited space for nonresidents. Smitty knew that UNC would be a long shot. No more than 18 percent of its freshman class could come from out of state. That made it even more difficult than the University of Virginia, which accepted about 30 percent from outside.

Some counselors were so careful about hurting feelings that families failed to hear the message. Smitty believed in the clear truth.

"Your son is not qualified to get in," he said. "Unless I'm missing something here. Did you or your husband go to Chapel Hill? Someone in the family is a major donor?"

No, the mother said, but her son belonged there. He wanted UNC, and she agreed.

Smitty was tempted to pull up the Naviance program to show her that other Oyster Bay kids with similar stats had little luck getting in. But he figured she would insist her son was different. Some parents were good at denial.

He decided to be as blunt as he could. "I guess you're determined to set your son up for a disappointment."

Smitty came to work before the start of school to meet with Riana's mother. He got right to the point, telling her about the crying episode in the hallway. For too long, Smitty assumed, Riana had bottled up all her anxieties because she didn't want to show any weakness.

"That's my daughter," the mom said.

Smitty said teachers had told him Riana was falling asleep in class. Matt Brown, too, sensed from Riana's appearance that she was in crisis. She had always been perfectly put together, but this week her hair had been mussed and her clothes wrinkled. Matt had told Riana to take some time off from the SADD activities; as president, she could delegate. So far she hadn't taken his advice.

Smitty told Riana's mom the girl had complained about clashes at home over curfews and many other issues.

Riana's stepfather loved her, the mom said, but both he and she believed in being strict. "I'm still Mom," she said, "and I still make the rules."

Yet she agreed Riana needed help. Did he have any ideas?

"If it's all right with you," Smitty said, "I'm going to talk to the manager of the drugstore. Maybe they can adjust her hours, or she can take a leave of absence until we get into December, when she has more time."

"Mr. Smith, I appreciate anything you can do," the mother said. "My daughter is strong willed. She doesn't want to be average. She wants to extend herself."

"A good quality, but we need to make sure she keeps on laughing, too."

Smitty invited Jeff's parents in for a conference, but first gave them an assignment: Draw a current family tree. Jeff had mentioned the sudden arrival of needy relatives. Who were they? "I'd like you to tell me who is living in the house and what their relationship is to you," he said.

Smitty often saw some of himself in Jeff. In high school, Smitty had captained the varsity basketball team and was voted "most popular"—a distinction that could also be applied to Jeff at Oyster Bay.

Smitty's oldest sister went to Boston University, his other sister graduated from Tufts, and their father was the superintendent of schools in their Maine community. It was a college town, next to the campus of Bowdoin, so his life was surrounded by education. But Smitty was not much of a student. Although he'd forgotten his SAT scores long ago, he doubted he broke 1050.

Jeff, he noted, had gotten 100 points higher than that. (Smitty took consolation from the fact that scores had been boosted in the 1990s when the test was "recentered.")

Just as Jeff seemed to be doing, Smitty decided on his career early. In middle school, he tagged along with one of his sisters when she met with her guidance director. The man's name, Mr. Tardy, seemed appropriate for someone who kept track of kids' attendance. Smitty admired Mr. Tardy's manner, and decided he'd like to be a counselor, too.

Smitty started his higher education at Hartwick, a respected college in upstate New York. For a history final, he memorized sixty-two pages of notes, then poured them back out on paper, thinking that would do. "If I get less than a ninety-seven, I'll eat the test," he boasted to his roommate. He got a D, and flunked out after a year. He realized he hadn't been a focused student, and cramming for tests without thinking about the material wasn't enough to compensate.

He moved back home for a year to work and take night courses at the University of Maine's extension center.

One of Smitty's best friends from Hartwick lived on Long Island and decided to transfer to Adelphi Suffolk College there, later known as Dowling. It was a commuter college whose campus was on a gracious one-time

Vanderbilt estate. The friend wanted Smitty to join him as a classmate—like the old days. Smitty was into the idea and started to apply, but the friend took matters into his own hands. He stopped by to see the director of admissions and pitched Smitty, saying he'd be a great addition to the student body. The director said he'd be happy to get a call from Smitty. The friend made that happen in a creative way. He walked to a pay phone and called the office again, this time claiming to be Smitty himself. He impersonated his friend's Down East accent during a "candidate's interview." It worked. At the end of the conversation, the admissions director congratulated Gwyeth Smith Jr. on his acceptance. After hearing what had happened, Smitty filed the needed paperwork, packed up, and moved to his third college in three years.

Early on, he still struggled. He spent his first semesters getting Bs and Cs. Then something in him woke up, and he started to deliver. During his last two years, Smitty became a student. He also began to consider his future. He got to know professors who worked as school counselors, and found a mentor in the admissions office.

The Adelphi Suffolk experience left him with an appreciation he might never have developed had he stayed at Hartwick. Schools don't need national status to have a lot to offer, and their students do just fine in life. One of Smitty's Adelphi Suffolk roommates lived in Singapore and became a Chevron general manager, another headed a major contracting company, a third published a novel, and a fourth helped run a big organization providing special education to school districts. Not bad, Smitty liked to say, for a bunch of guys from a commuter school.

Over the years, Smitty steered many boys and girls to places like his alma mater. He placed others in community colleges, culinary schools, vocational institutes, even programs that trained golf pros. For some, these places fit their interests; for others with learning disabilities or poor study habits, it's where they were likeliest to find success. When parents hesitated, he assured them their kids would do well—not everyone, he said, was meant to go to mainstream colleges, and he'd point to himself as an example.

Although Smitty was one of the best-known people in Oyster Bay, hardly anyone realized that the guidance guru had once flunked out of college. Nor did they know that he'd gone through three campuses before earning his bachelor's degree. Smitty didn't hide any of that, and was happy to talk about it when asked, but generally it wasn't relevant. His friend Matt Brown considered it a positive. He sensed that Smitty's own journey left him with a soft spot for "youngstahs" who had focus issues or family distractions, like Jeff, for example, or Riana—two kids who had a lot to offer.

Jeff Sanders's mom and dad sat down in Smitty's office. They took out the family tree he'd requested. Then Jeff's father started to talk about his son.

"Jeff's a great kid," he said. "Has always been a great kid."

He was industrious, too. When he was eight, the dad recalled, he went to a stationery and candy store to ask for a job. The owner told him to try when he was older. But Jeff wouldn't take a no. He offered to stock shelves in return for payment in candy, and the owner finally agreed. Jeff was so convincing that he got his teenage sister a job, too.

Jeff's father flashed forward to the family's current situation. Yes, he said, a lot of complicated situations had brought needy relatives into their home. Jeff's uncle had died about three years earlier after taking drugs. Jeff's aunt, who had been in and out of drug treatment, was not qualified to take care of their three children, ages four to twelve, so Jeff's family temporarily took them in. They hoped the aunt would be back on her feet soon, but she wasn't yet.

"My sister-in-law has been through seven or eight rehabs of one type or another in the last three years," the dad explained.

In short, Jeff's parents said, these three kids would likely be with them for a long time.

Smitty took notes and kept listening.

"Jeff was fourteen when they came," the father continued. "His brother had moved out and he had just gotten a room to himself. It was just going to be us and him. It was going to be a whole different life for him."

And then this. Jeff's father was in the insurance business and worked days. Jeff's mother, a nurse, worked nights. Both said their son had been extraordinary through all the changes. "Jeff really stepped up because there was a lot of child care to be done," the dad said. "A lot of Friday nights when he wanted to be somewhere else he was home watching the kids."

Smitty shook his head in wonder. "I didn't know this."

The mom nodded. Her son was the kind to keep it inside. "Jeff doesn't want to be perceived as needing pity," she said. "He fights it."

Smitty was still trying to do the math. "Three of you plus three of them," he said of the children. But he knew there were more. "Who else lives in the house?"

They said they had—believe it or not—a second sister-in-law, who was recovering from a tough divorce. She had two sons. All three were living in the basement.

That made six relatives in addition to Jeff and his parents. "That's nine," Smitty said, counting from his notes. He would need an exact number when he wrote a recommendation letter, and again in January when he helped Jeff's parents with financial aid forms.

"Who else?"

"Jeff's grandmother, who lives with us, suffered a stroke a while ago," the mother said.

"Ten people," said Smitty.

"I have a brother-in-law who is in a wheelchair from a car accident," the father said.

"Eleven," Smitty counted.

He had two aides who did twelve-hour shifts.

"Thirteen," Smitty said.

And Jeff's brother had moved back in.

Fourteen. No wonder Jeff couldn't study much at home.

Jeff's father said that he and his wife had put an addition on their house.

"You folks are inspiring," Smitty remarked.

"There's always somebody with a worse story than yours," the mom pointed out.

"Our life would be simpler if it wasn't for these events," added Jeff's dad. "We would just have Jeff, who is—knock on wood—an all-star kid."

Smitty liked that phrase. And as Jeff's counselor, he couldn't help but think this crisis could also be a positive part of Jeff's college quest. The parents had given him plenty to show admissions offices that Jeff would bring a lot to a campus.

ELEVEN

Strategizing

On a rainy autumn afternoon, Smitty stood with a wet coat and dripping umbrella in the back of a drugstore, waiting for the manager. It was the store where Riana worked too many hours for a full-time senior applying to college. Smitty had decided he had a better chance of fixing that in person than he would over the phone.

He often made outside visits for kids—calling on one in a psychiatric ward after a bipolar episode, another in a treatment center after an overdose, and a third in the ER after his football season had been ruined by a broken bone. Now he was in aisle 1 standing by the Oil of Olay display.

Soon, the manager emerged from her office. Smitty introduced himself as head of guidance at Oyster Bay High School. He said he was here about Riana Tyson. He was concerned her schedule was too much for her and hoped the manager could offer her a break.

"She's a bright youngster struggling with her workload," he explained.

"I realize that's not your issue and I don't want to inconvenience you." But he asked if she'd consider reducing Riana's hours for a few weeks.

The manager praised Riana for being a good employee and agreed to try, as long as all shifts were covered.

Smitty wasn't accepting "maybe." "This young lady is taking four AP courses," he said, almost pleading, "and we've got to make sure she does the schoolwork she's required to do."

The manager explained that employees had to work at least ten hours a week to stay on the computerized payroll.

Smitty had never been shy about suggesting solutions. He didn't feel it was enough to ask people to just do their best. He proposed that instead of working evenings during the week, Riana do four hours on Fridays and six on Sundays. That way, she'd have time to focus on school when she needed to while still meeting the store's time quota.

The manager considered it briefly, and said that would be fine.

Smitty thanked her and asked for her boss's name so he could send a letter of appreciation. As he stepped out, he raised his hands in bemusement.

"Don't you love this technological age? You don't exist in their computer if you can't work at least ten hours."

Back at school a few minutes later, he called Riana's mother to share the news. He would soon tell Riana that she'd have time to get her applications done.

When considering a student's college choices, Smitty liked to step back and think not just about the school but about larger questions. If a kid wanted to apply somewhere early decision, Smitty would ask if he'd really be ready to commit by December. Where money was an issue, wouldn't it be better to wait and compare financial aid offers from several colleges in the spring?

He liked to do tactical thinking as well.

If a girl was considering a college that had a shortage of male students, would she be ready for an admissions process that would likely hold females to a higher standard? Similarly, might some science-oriented girls be better directed toward schools looking for women to round out their engineering program?

If a girl was enamored of Columbia, why not apply to Barnard, the women's school where the odds of admission are higher but students have access to Columbia's courses, dining halls, and libraries?

What if a poli-sci kid wanted to go to Cornell, but was a long shot as a mainstream arts-and-sciences applicant? Might he find a better chance, and a good fit, applying to Cornell's Industrial and Labor Relations school?

Smitty tried to get the kids to do such strategic thinking. If there was a helpful tactic, why not use it?

Many of Smitty's kids said they wanted to major in psychology—a popular choice because teens like the idea of analyzing themselves. But Smitty advised them to carefully consider their interests to avoid appearing like stereotypical adolescents. "Psychology is such a popular major that it takes away from your uniqueness," he reasoned. He sometimes gave the same advice about biology, often the default major for premeds. If you're truly passionate about biology, he told kids, then do declare it your intended major—but first make sure your transcripts and extracurriculars show you're serious. Yet he also knew that if someone candidly puts "undecided" as a major, admissions officers often worry that he or she is undefined.

From time to time, Smitty sat with one of the other two counselors, "Smitty's angels," to review cases. The sessions would range from general philosophy to individual strategy. "Think about an application like a business plan," Smitty told Deanna one day as they sat at the round table. "You emphasize what you do well."

He changed the subject to tests. It was an area most parents didn't fully understand. Many, he said, had taken the SAT as teenagers, so they knew the top score for each section was 800. But they were less familiar with the ACT, which had a maximum of 36.

Smitty looked at the files of a girl who wanted to study engineering at either Delaware or Stony Brook, which had a Women in Science and Engineering program. Her SATs were good but not great: 1220. Her ACT composite was 28.

Smitty kept an SAT-ACT conversion chart next to his computer, but rarely referred to it because he knew it by heart. "That 28 is the equivalent of 1260 on the SAT," he told Deanna. He recommended the girl send in her more impressive ACT number and hold back her SATs.

Smitty found the SAT less a measure of intelligence than of a student's knack for test taking. He thought the ACT was a better gauge of mastery of a subject. Although used more in the West and Midwest, the ACT was gaining in the East, and Smitty was one of the counselors behind its growing popularity.

Over the years, Smitty had often expressed concerns to officials of the College Board, which administered the SAT. He felt the test was biased toward rich kids who could take the best prep courses. Recently, the College Board had ruled that those who take the SAT multiple times can send in only their best scores. Smitty felt that also favored affluent kids, who could afford to keep redoing the test. He'd worked in several districts with many such students, so it helped their cause—and his. But his instinct for fairness made him no fan of the SAT.

Smitty saw other problems with the SAT culture. Too often, he thought, students feel pressure to take the test before they're ready, sometimes early in their junior year. The girl who wanted to be an engineer did exactly that with the SAT Math I—one of the Subject Tests, formerly called SAT IIs. The regular SATs—math, English, and writing—are called the Reasoning Tests. The Subject Tests are an additional measure to show a high level of knowledge by students who have taken multiple college prep classes. The would-be engineer hadn't done enough of that. She had impressive grades, but her SAT Math I score came in at a low 490, hurting her record.

"Why the heck she ever took that test in January of eleventh grade is beyond me," Smitty told Deanna. He felt the girl should have waited to finish more prep classes in the spring. The 490, he said, put her in the lower 50 percent of performers—"the kiss of death at a good engineering school."

"What should we do?" Deanna asked.

"Don't send out her results," said Smitty. The good news, he added, was that Delaware and Penn State don't require an SAT Subject Test. As for Stony Brook, the test is recommended but not required.

Deanna asked how he knew that kind of detail.

"I'm old," he replied, smiling.

Smitty's time in admissions boot camp reminded him that selective colleges are looking for any reason to weed out applicants. If you don't need to, why give them a reason? If, however, you do have to report a fluke bad score that unfairly taints a smart kid, it is important to give an explanation.

Smitty reminded Deanna about a girl who'd graduated in June with impeccable grades. But she had panic attacks when she took standardized tests, and hadn't managed to break a 1250 on the SATs. On other tests, he said, she was all over the place, with an impressive 5 on her AP bio exam and a lowly 1 on AP chem. Smitty explained her test phobia in his letter to the University of Chicago, where she wanted to go into premed. Colleges, Smitty had found, do understand that some bright students can stumble on tests. She was admitted.

Next, he and Deanna examined the file of a kid who wanted to be a large-animal veterinarian. Her composite ACT was 29, equivalent to a 1300. Yet her SAT was only a 1250. "Another ACT kid," he said. And another reason Smitty didn't love the SAT. She was interested in Penn State or Cornell's School of Agriculture. He said that boded well. Both of those schools were looking for students who wanted to be large-animal vets.

Deanna wondered how Smitty came up with these facts. She started to ask: "How do you . . ." Then she paused, smiled, and answered herself. "Oh, right. You're old."

The third and final case was that of twin brothers. The class also had a set of twin sisters. Smitty, connoisseur of Oyster Bay trivia, remarked that the twin brothers had taken the twin sisters to the junior prom. "You gotta love this place," he said.

Back to business. The brothers were both applying early to Vanderbilt. Smitty knew that one, trying for the competitive engineering program, had a 32 on the ACT. "Excellent," Smitty said. "The ninety-ninth percentile. Equivalent to 1420 on the SAT."

"But his SATs don't even come close to that," Deanna responded. "He's got a 1280."

Again, Smitty said they should send only the ACT score. Smitty looked at the boy's transcript: three AP courses, two honors, and Regents tests in the high nineties.

"He's in."

"What?"

"I bet he'll get into Vandy."

"How can you—" Again, Deanna stopped, and this time just smiled.

"No problem with those numbers," Smitty said of the boy. "The difficult piece is what'll happen to his brother."

The twins' GPAs were almost identical, but their scores weren't. The other brother's highest SAT composite was 1200, and his best ACT total was a 28, the ninety-second percentile. Normally, that might count him out, but Smitty knew that many schools didn't like to accept one twin and turn down the other. "Usually," he said, "the admissions person is thinking, 'If I want one, how do I find a way to justify taking his twin?'"

Smitty told Deanna to emphasize in each recommendation letter that the applicant had a twin applying. Then he sighed and observed out loud the cost of putting twins through four years of a school like Vanderbilt—more than $400,000.

The meeting ended and the two went back to work.

Chelsea floated into Smitty's office one fall day to talk about Skidmore. He thought the school could be ideal for her. Tucked into the hills of Saratoga Springs, it attracted creative kids. It had no math or science requirements. Smitty didn't believe in college rankings, but anyone who did would note that Skidmore consistently made the *Princeton Review*'s top-twenty list of "Birkenstock-wearing, tree-hugging, clove-smoking vegetarians."

Yet Smitty was anxious about Chelsea's chances of getting in. Skidmore had a 61-39 female-to-male ratio. That imbalance was a problem at some colleges, and was especially acute at places like Skidmore that used to be all female. A recent study had found, perhaps predictably, that at schools with a 60-40 imbalance, males had a better chance of getting in than females with the same qualifications.

Chelsea's 1300 SAT composite was fine, but it wasn't going to astound anyone at Skidmore, where admitted kids scored about 1320.

"What else is on your list?" Smitty asked her.

To his relief, she was still intrigued by Charleston, and was considering Tulane and the University of Vermont. Middlebury, although tougher, also made the list.

Yet Skidmore was still her likely preference at this point. Smitty worried she could be headed for disappointment. Sometimes, his job was to coax a student to prefer a place with better odds.

Smitty usually debriefed two or three teachers before writing a student's recommendation letter, but he knew Allyson Frankel well enough to begin on his own.

"Friends describe her as someone who is crazy, unique, and helpful," he wrote, "a loyal friend who is sought after for advice, and someone who is uplifting." Allyson couldn't signal her enthusiasm for Michigan by applying early action or early decision because the school didn't offer those options. But Smitty could make it clear, and he did:

"She has visited universities that are as different as Michigan, the University of Chicago, Emory, and Northwestern," he wrote, "and has decided that Michigan provides the environment that will challenge her."

He usually avoided targeting a recommendation letter to one particular college—he worried a clerical glitch could end up sending it to the wrong school. He'd made that mistake a few years earlier when he mailed Yale a letter that told of a student's passion for Lafayette. A Yale admissions officer called, laughing, to tell him what he'd done. In any case, Yale was a stretch for this kid, who ultimately didn't get in.

When he thought about Allyson, Smitty sometimes recalled an essay her sister had written a few years before about a vacation on a sailboat. The essay started with nice descriptions of the trip, but then went too far trying to dramatically paint it as a life-changing experience.

"I'm not sure how to approach you," Smitty had said. "Do I need to be gentle?"

Allyson's sister laughed. "No, Mr. Smith. Cut right to it."

"This essay sucks."

He explained: "Young people believe they need to write about things that are earthshaking, but the reader wants to get a better feel for what's in your soul."

This year, fortunately, Allyson, in meeting her self-inflicted deadline, had nailed the essays. Her Common App piece on an extracurricular activity was about a tennis match:

We hammered, stroked, slammed, whipped, and dashed. Muscles aching and minds racing, it all came down to this one point. "Deuce!" Winner takes all.

I toss the yellow rocket into the air; I feel her stare. She may be bigger, she may be stronger, but I want this more. The ball flies into the air, and with one swift motion, I whip my racket. I live for moments like this.

In the first drafts, Kathi had red-lined Allyson's adjectives—*crisp* air, *relentless* passion, *intense* determination; and her adverbs—*forcefully* whip, *painfully* tense. Allyson by now knew the less-is-more rule. She deleted them.

Smitty was impressed that Allyson had described something small without trying to make it a metaphor for overcoming obstacles. This was a rare essay about sports that worked because it didn't try to be an essay about life.

She also wrote about her fund-raising effort, emphasizing the human rights problems in Darfur, not the amount of money raised.

Allyson had handled the admissions game the way Smitty liked kids to play. She'd researched Michigan, she'd weighed rolling admissions versus early decision, and she'd sent her application in October. She was already working on the apps for Emory, Wisconsin, Indiana, and BU in case she needed backups.

More significant to Smitty, Allyson had made plans for another Darfur fund-raising concert in the spring—long after admissions offices would know or care about her activities.

If this girl didn't get into one of her top choices, Smitty thought, then something was wrong with the system.

TWELVE

The GPA Game

"Show, don't tell," Smitty liked to say, and one blustery evening he followed his own advice. Standing on the stage of Oyster Bay's auditorium before ninth and tenth graders and their parents, he asked for eight student volunteers. Much of the audience was new to the world of college admissions. Smitty was about to give them a glimpse of it.

Most, of course, knew that getting in was about grades and scores. He wanted them to see that plenty of other factors came into play as well. He gave each of the volunteers a big card with a grade point average in large black numbers on the front and a list of individual characteristics on the back. He lined up the kids shoulder to shoulder—a boy holding up a 4.0 GPA, a girl with a 3.7 next to him, another with 3.3, and so on. The audience could see the numbers, but nothing else. He had them all start on the same line on the stage, facing forward. No one yet had an edge.

Smitty, playing the role of the admissions dean, began calling out instructions in a deep voice. "If you have taken an exceptionally strong academic program, move forward two spaces." A couple of kids shuffled closer to the audience.

"If you direct the gospel choir at your church, move up one space." One student took a step.

By now, the crowd was fully engaged, particularly the parents.

"You clearly stated that this college is your choice by making an early decision application and commitment, move forward two spaces."

The next one surprised some folks. "Your intended major is psychology or biology, move back one space."

Smitty paused before he read each instruction, letting the "applicants" move into new spots.

"If your intended major is Greek, move forward one space."

Some characteristics had a bigger impact than folks expected: "If you do not know any of your teachers well enough to feel comfortable asking for a recommendation, move back two spaces." A couple of kids faded back.

His next instruction was delivered lightly, but it addressed a mistake Oyster Bay students made too frequently. "If, when you word-processed your application essay, you forgot to change the name of the college you were applying to, move back three spaces." There was nervous laughter as the relevant players retreated.

"You are a legacy—a legacy means your mother or father attended the college to which you are applying—move forward two spaces." Two students did. Smitty waited for everyone to take in the changes so far.

"The topic of your essay is sports as a metaphor for life, move back one space." Two students dropped back, to more laughter.

"You wrote the essay of the year—the one everyone passed around the office—move forward two spaces."

He lowered his voice. "If you plagiarized an American history paper and got caught—" He waited again for effect, then his voice boomed, "Sit down. You're out of the competition altogether!" Down went the boy with the 3.3.

This was his first time doing the demonstration, known as the GPA Game. He'd learned it a year earlier while teaching a graduate school counseling course on the side at nearby Long Island University. A friend from Columbia's admissions office who had done the exercise elsewhere came in to show it to Smitty's class.

Smitty liked it so much he decided to use it on this night. He felt it would paint a better picture than a simple admissions lecture.

"If you will be the first in your family to attend college, move forward two spaces." By now, the 4.0 and 3.7 students had fallen back. The audience was seeing that it wasn't all about scores.

"If you have participated in no extracurricular activities, move back three spaces."

Smitty peered at the crowd to make sure they were paying attention to the final sets of instructions. "If you have participated in a *significant* community project, move forward one space."

"If you are . . ." Smitty paused again, "an Eagle Scout or a Gold Award recipient"—the equivalent for girls—"move forward two spaces."

He stepped up the pace.

"Varsity athlete, move forward one space."

"All-region in a sport, move up another space."

He issued this stark warning: "If you got a D in an academic course at the end of junior year, move back three spaces."

Followed by some hope: "If you wrote a letter to a college admissions officer and explained the extenuating circumstances for that D, move forward one space."

Some of those with the top grades weren't doing well and one was about to do even worse: "If you decided to protect your GPA by not taking AP courses, move back two spaces." The boy with the 4.0 stepped back.

"If you come from a single-parent household and must work part-time to help with expenses, move forward two spaces."

It was time for the final factor.

"If your last name is Bush, and the name of the college library is Bush, and it's not a coincidence"—this brought chuckles—"move all the way to the front of the line and stay there."

Smitty looked over the audience as the results sank in. Students with the lowest averages were toward the back, which made sense, but the 4.0 student was now several steps from the front of the line. The cheater was seated.

"Take a look," Smitty said, gesturing at the seven students who remained standing. "Note that it's the 3.7 and the 3.5 who got in."

While watching the exercise, Smitty thought back to some of the seniors he'd been working with: Jeff's disappointing grades junior year; Allyson's fund-raising for Darfur; Riana about to fulfill her mother's dreams of college; and Colin, who'd been recruited for crew. Another boy, Curtis, had suffered meningitis as a child, and had undergone surgery several times. During the ordeal, his father had left home and disappeared, so Curtis worked to help pay the bills.

Smitty wrapped up the GPA Game, emphasizing its main lesson:

"Admissions goes beyond pure numbers. You want your youngster to be a very serious student, but to have time for service, a sport, a fun activity."

A few of the parents looked more unnerved than reassured. Smitty tried again.

"Colleges want balance in your children, just as you do."

For Smitty, one of the most important gauges of a student's readiness for college was the Time Use Test, or TUT. It measured the way kids spent their days. Someone who played video games five hours a day scored low.

With all his activities in school and in the Korean community, Lee Kim was almost off the TUT scale. And he'd taken on an additional activity recently: He was going to be a star in the student production of *Little Shop of Horrors*. Day after day, he stood in a music classroom, singing, then yelling, "Feed me, Seymour!" in his deep voice.

And yet, of all people, Lee frittered away time when he was supposed to be doing applications. A week before the Oxford deadline, he didn't know if the admissions office needed to see his Regents scores. His personal essay was far longer than Oxford's five-thousand-character maximum. And he wasn't even sure how many recommendations were required.

By this point in October, geese were flying south over the harbor every few days; Smitty could hear them from room 207. They were a reminder that college applicants had better start hustling.

"Which teachers have you asked for recommendations?" Smitty inquired.

Lee almost seemed to shrug. "None."

S mitty enjoyed working with what he called the specialists. Most kids took part in an extracurricular activity; the specialists had major talent. They were the ones likely to play sports in college or go to drama or music school.

Dominique was one. An asuring actress, she was applying to Juilliard, which had an acceptance rate of 7.7 percent—lower than Harvard. Juilliard's drama program was even more exclusive: According to the school's Web site, one thousand candidates competed for about eighteen places in each year's freshman class.

Smitty knew Dominique's prospects would hinge on the brief auditions she performed in January. She had to memorize four monologues—and for other theater schools, still more monologues, some from Shakespeare, and others from Greek drama.

In essay class, Dominique talked with Lee about the stress of the audition process. Some colleges, she said, made you perform in large, near-empty theaters. It was intentionally intimidating. Plus, there's the competition—so many kids, she said, for so few spots. She told Lee that deep down no one wishes you well. "While you wait," she said, "you have all the other actors sitting in the hallways saying nice things to you but wanting to gouge your eyes out."

Dominique, a brunette with an average build, had recently visited Juilliard. She met a rival applicant there who gave her one of those smiling digs. "Don't worry," the rival said merrily, "they're looking for a skinny blond."

The conspiracies of drama students, Smitty liked to say, paled next to those of college coaches. Well, that was overstating it; the vast majority played fair, but a few of Smitty's kids had been burned by a few coaches who didn't. Three years before, an outstanding Oyster Bay tennis player had planned to attend the University of Pennsylvania's Wharton School. His head got turned when he was suddenly courted by Harvard's coach. The athletic liaison at Harvard told Smitty the school loved the kid. So the boy applied early. Not all coaches can guarantee admission to an athlete, but when one says he wants you, and tells you he can see you on his team, that's code for, *You're in.* Not in this case. Oyster Bay's tennis star was stunned when Harvard deferred him. Smitty heard that another top-seeded player had become available. He recontacted Penn's coach, who angrily told Smitty the boy had lost his chance.

Smitty wasn't going to let it drop. He e-mailed Harvard's coach to say the school had misled the boy. "I allowed myself to believe that all those recruiting nightmares could not occur at a school such as Harvard," Smitty wrote. It made no difference, but Smitty hoped the coach would think before misleading another seventeen-year-old in the future. Meanwhile, Smitty made a flurry of calls to tennis coaches, and the boy got into Brown. The next year, Smitty and Kathi went to see the team play in an Ivy League championship. "They destroyed Harvard," Smitty recalled with satisfaction.

This year, Smitty was keeping an eye out for a couple of senior athletes. Tara, one of the twin girls, was a nationally ranked soccer player. A coach at Clemson had recruited her, and she was set to go—but the coach suddenly announced he was leaving. That could leave a recruited athlete off the radar screen, so Smitty thought Tara should keep looking.

Smitty also was watching out for Colin, the senior with the 1460 SAT score who was a top crew recruit. Colin had attracted the interest of Princeton, Yale, Harvard, and Dartmouth. His family didn't ask the guidance department for a lot of help, and Smitty thought that was fine. Sometimes, especially with athletes, the process comes to them, with colleges chasing the student rather than the other way around. Coaches will call out of the blue asking a prospect to apply, and soon you have a ready-made list.

On an October weekend, Colin visited Dartmouth. When he returned, he e-mailed Smitty to say he'd had a great trip and wanted to apply early decision. He was ready to make a commitment.

Smitty asked Colin to hold off. He called the Dartmouth coach.

"I don't mean to be presumptuous," Smitty said. "Colin was impressed by his visit. Loved your school. Loved you guys more than that, and just thought it was a great fit. . . ."

The coach asked if there was a problem.

"My only reservation—and it has nothing to do with Dartmouth, believe me—is sometimes kids make knee-jerk decisions when they're emotionally high or when they're down in the dumps."

Smitty explained that he'd had a bad experience with a recruited tennis player a few years earlier. "A kid got caught in a situation that was just unethical, it was ugly, it just wasn't right."

At that point, Smitty got the information he was looking for. The crew coach said he was seriously considering ten boys. Colin was in the top five.

"That's helpful to me, Coach," Smitty remarked. "It really is."

A few minutes later Colin stopped by. Smitty told him the good news, but still asked him to spend a couple of days thinking before sending his application. This was early decision, so if he got accepted he'd be bound to say no to Yale, Princeton, or Harvard if they came calling. Colin agreed to wait, but he told Smitty he'd already made up his mind.

On October 15, Oxford's deadline day, Lee sat muttering in room 207, pasting text into the British version of the Common Application. The night before, he'd realized that he needed to send two of his graded papers. He didn't like anything he'd done so far in senior year, so he printed out two essays from junior year and cajoled the English teacher to mark them up and grade them again since he'd lost the originals.

Even as he filled out the application, he couldn't get excited about it. He wondered if he really needed college at all. Maybe he would be better off traveling or working instead.

Lee was still trying to sort out his parents' desire for him to get ahead and his own desire to get away. He wanted to be independent, yet still felt the call to be a "good son"—one who gets a fine education, then returns home to help his parents.

"A good son," Lee would say, "isn't some guy who goes away and makes a shitload of money."

The Oxford essay gave him a chance to write his thoughts, and as the deadline approached, he finally captured them on-screen:

At the end of the day, I always question myself: What is it all for? Why bother going through the college application process anyway? In this vast universe, what is it that is so amazing about me that will be remembered? I'm no different than the other 6.7 billion people on this blue marble floating through space. Am I?

He kept writing. Every few minutes he'd call out a question to Kathi: "'Silence *seemed* deafening' or 'silence *was* deafening'?"

"'*Was* deafening.'"

"Do British people understand 'break the ice'?"

"Guess it's better than 'stepping up to the plate,'" she said.

Although Lee felt that getting into Oxford wouldn't quell his doubts about college, it had the prestige to make his parents happy.

At last, with the clock ticking, he finished the application and rushed down the stairs to Smitty's office. Because of the time difference in England, the deadline was just a few minutes away. Smitty barely had a chance to proofread it.

The fax whirred and Lee was done. His application, and his fate, now lay on the other side of the ocean.

THIRTEEN

"We're Looking for the X Factor"

For years, the SAT had been *the* test at Oyster Bay High for kids going to college. On a drizzly, muggy Saturday four days before Halloween in 2007, it finally faced some competition. For the first time, Oyster Bay was going to be a test center for the ACT, which had long been a rarity in the Northeast. Smitty wanted to break the SAT monopoly. Although he wasn't a fan of standardized testing, he knew it wasn't going away. A growing camp had argued that ACTs were better at measuring what kids learned in high school. Smitty was among them. In his mind, this wasn't just a technical debate. These tests had a huge impact on the lives of American high school students, so he was thrilled to see the ACT establish a beachhead at Oyster Bay.

The students seemed less enamored. Kids trudged into the school, their damp hair adding to the air of resignation. Curtis, who had undergone several operations on his leg, was the first to arrive, at 7:39 A.M. He carried a bag of snacks and a calculator. Allyson, wearing an Indiana sweatshirt and munching an apple, walked in a couple of minutes later.

Then came three inseparable girls known as the Three Amigas, followed by Riana, wearing sweatpants and wiping the sleep from her eyes.

Smitty had a good view of it all because he was serving as test administrator. He was glad the exam was being offered right here, as opposed to other nearby schools. It gave his kids a home-court advantage. They'd feel more comfortable taking it in a setting they knew well. Smitty felt in some cases that could be worth extra points. Also, since they wouldn't have to drive to another center, kids could get extra sleep and show up in time for the eight o'clock start.

Except for Chelsea, who hadn't arrived by 7:56, even though she lived across the street.

She was among those most on his mind today. If Chelsea could get a 30 or above—which Smitty considered likely—her ACT score would be better than her 1300 SATs. That would help her at tough schools like NYU and Middlebury. But as Smitty sat looking over the administrator's 114-page guide to running the test, he didn't see her. Where was she?

S mitty had been trying for years to get Oyster Bay to run testing more responsibly. They did hold SAT exams at the school, but for years they'd seemed to oversee them in a casual way. He felt they'd skimped on money in administering tests. At one point a few years before, he met with the superintendent about it. Smitty began their chat with a line he hoped would dramatize his point.

"I'm glad we're a school that puts such a premium on athletics," he said. Smitty pointed out that the district paid teachers overtime to be scorekeepers at athletic games, while using less-experienced, lower-paid paraprofessionals and lunch aides to monitor the SAT. They didn't know the students well, and he worried that some kids might think they could play loose with the rules.

"It's a disaster waiting to happen," Smitty warned.

He'd seen problems elsewhere. At a district where he once worked, the SAT was disrupted when kids talked and switched seats. Afterward, some students complained, and a week later, College Board officials arrived from their Princeton, New Jersey, headquarters in a white limousine. They did an investigation and announced they were invalidating all the tests given at the school that day. Smitty didn't protest. In fact, he'd written a memo before the problem calling for safeguards. After that, his suggestions were finally followed, as they were now on this Saturday at Oyster Bay as the ACT got off to a good start.

Three minutes before the ACT was to begin, Chelsea dashed up to Smitty and told him she didn't want to take the test. She'd been so busy with schoolwork and college visits that she hadn't prepared.

Smitty respected her hesitancy.

"Got to listen to your gut," he said.

Chelsea kept making her case, as if she expected him to say no.

"Mr. Smith, it's just that I need to study for it."

He said reassuringly, "Good decision."

Chelsea promised to take it in two months, in December. Smitty had no problem with that. In the 1990s, his own daughter, Nicole, had been ranked third at one of Long Island's most prestigious high schools. She'd taken the SAT and ACT and done well. But she wanted to go to Harvard and Smitty felt she should do the exams again to show she could do better still. A bit to his surprise, she told him she just wasn't up for it. She was all tested out. Smitty understood. He believed kids sometimes needed to be pushed, but not always into things they didn't *have* to do. Now, after graduating from Duke and Rutgers, than becoming a college professor, Nicole said she never regretted the decision to skip another round of testing.

He thought of Nicole as he chatted briefly with Chelsea. Perhaps, come December, she would hesitate again and decide against taking the ACT altogether. If so, he would support her. She'd done well enough on the SATs. If some colleges couldn't see her creativity and chose other applicants based on scores alone, well, that was their loss.

I t's a fall ritual for college admissions reps to visit high schools and make a pitch. Smitty invited as many as he could to Oyster Bay. He knew that when they sat to read folders, they would likely remember the school and its applicants. It's one of those factors you can't measure, but Smitty understood it could only bring alive a paper application.

Smitty made sure that George Washington University always stopped by, in part because one of its top admissions people, Michael O'Leary, was a 1979 grad of Oyster Bay. Smitty would chat with him about how Oyster Bay had come up from a low-key school in a sleepy hamlet to a more high-powered institution that could compete with big rivals like Jericho—but still keep its community feel. Almost every year, several of Smitty's kids were accepted and headed off to GWU.

Oyster Bay didn't attract the same number of prestige-school reps as its neighbors, so when an Ivy admissions officer showed up it was an event. One morning in October, Columbia came to call. The session was held in a conference room and drew ten kids—several far better dressed than usual.

By Smitty's count, eight definitely intended to apply to Columbia. Three of them were going early: Adati, who wanted to be a surgeon and whose parents were immigrants from India; Zara, who wanted to study law and came from a family from Bangladesh; and Nathaniel, newly focused on Columbia because his previous choice, MIT, required too many essays.

Nathaniel, perhaps even more than the others, was feeling tense about his early bid. His mother had helped him choose colleges with top engineering programs, and made it clear she hoped for a yes from this one. Sometimes Smitty felt the mom cared more about a Columbia acceptance than Nathaniel did.

When the kids settled around a table, the Columbia rep spoke with a New Yorker's speed, describing a nonstop campus with need blind admissions, guaranteed housing, and no classes on Fridays. He mentioned that Columbia had four-hundred clubs for students, and hundreds of other extracurricular offerings. It was a place for kids who had abundant interests.

"You're going to have New York City as your playground," he said. "It's not the same as being in a school surrounded by cows."

Lee Kim, who was considering a college on a California ranch surrounded by cows, seemed intrigued nonetheless.

The rep offered a tip about the essay. "Please make sure you do not write, 'I'm applying to Columbia because it's an Ivy League school in New York City.' That's the easiest way to anger the admissions committee."

The kids laughed. Smitty suspected at least one had been planning on writing that very sentence.

Smitty spoke up suddenly from the back of the conference room: "Is there anybody here who doesn't swim?"

The kids looked at him quizzically.

Smitty explained: Columbia, Harvard, and a few other colleges wouldn't let students earn a diploma until they'd passed a swim test. It was a tradition that stretched back for decades.

The rep nodded. "Students realize in April of their senior year you really have to jump into the pool to graduate from Columbia," he said. The kids laughed.

The visitor tried to reassure the kids that Columbia wasn't only about scores. He said the admissions staff could fill the freshman class three times over just with valedictorians and salutatorians. But they wanted more variety.

A few kids glanced at Layla and Jenna, Oyster Bay's valedictorian and salutatorian. The two kept their gazes on the rep.

He continued: "I like to say the easiest person *not* to admit to Columbia is someone who has a 107.35 GPA, 2400 SATs, and does absolutely nothing." In his own way, the rep was repeating one of the lessons of the GPA Game. "We're looking for the X factor," he told them.

He went on to say that Columbia didn't limit the number of students admitted from a particular high school. He looked at the ten boys and girls in the conference room. "Don't worry if everyone around this table submits an application to Columbia. It's possible everyone could be admitted."

He added, "It's possible no one could be admitted."

A bit harsh perhaps, but it struck Smitty this was another benefit of a visit by a college rep. The good ones offered not just encouragement but a dose of reality. A college rejection, he knew, would be one of the great disappointments in the lives of many of these youngsters. Maybe it wouldn't sting as much if they heard firsthand just how tough the odds could be.

FOURTEEN

Essay Therapy

Many days, Essay Writing for College seemed more like group therapy than an English class. One kid wrote about a parent's battle with depression, and another about a schizophrenic family member. A girl described being a child of divorce, then helped her best friend write an essay about her own parents' divorce.

But another camp made it clear they wouldn't focus on hardships. Jeff had no intention of writing about his relatives' drug problems or the cousins taken into his house. He was private about it, and besides, it might come off as self-pity, which wasn't his style. Curtis had contracted meningitis in elementary school, almost lost his leg, and was still having surgeries to correct the damage. Kids knew that much about him. Most didn't know that his father had vanished. Curtis spoke about his dad reverently, so Smitty was all but certain Curtis wouldn't write about that.

Kasper was the chattiest one in class, but avoided mentioning his own dad, who had been killed by a train in August. Smitty decided not to push him to write about it; the tragedy was too recent and Kasper might not be ready.

After nearly four decades as a school counselor, Smitty was still surprised by the upheavals teenagers faced. In every community where he'd worked, rich or poor, kids were dealing with what some counselors called the Ds: death, disease, divorce, debt, drink, drugs, depression, and disorders.

Smitty and Kathi once began counting up the seniors who faced such issues. They stopped when they reached twenty-four—about a quarter of the class. Smitty often encouraged kids to write about these ordeals, both for a strong application and to help them sort it out.

He recognized these were serious matters for seventeen-year-olds, so some days, he asked Matt Brown for advice on how to help.

Matt told him that almost by definition, students this age are in crisis, and if they weren't now, they could be by the time they got to college. "High school seniors," Matt said, "have conflicting feelings about staying home or leaving home, growing up or holding on to their childhoods."

As a social worker, Matt supported essays on such matters for a pragmatic reason. He felt it would help kids know themselves, and perhaps as a result, make more thoughtful choices about school picks, majors, and even careers.

Sometimes Smitty pushed hard for kids to be honest about inner issues. The year before, he'd done that with Brady, who had gone on to study engineering at Rice. Brady first wrote an impersonal essay about pitching on the baseball team.

"Where are *you* in this essay?" Smitty asked. He suggested Brady explore the central event in his life—the death of his father during surgery two years earlier. Brady resisted. Smitty nudged him, and Brady agreed to try. The early drafts were superficial. At one point, Smitty worried he'd gone overboard when Brady walked out of the classroom in tears. But

Brady went back to writing, and kept going through six drafts. Kathi liked the final piece so much she decided to read it to this year's seniors.

Brady began by saying that after the loss, he wasn't comfortable showing emotions. He pretended he was fine even when he was falling apart inside. But his grades dropped and he lost interest in things. Kathi liked the way he used unexpected details: "I couldn't fathom a life without my father," he wrote. "I was angry at everything around me, angry at the weather, angry at the TV, angry at the alarm clock."

Then he told of an awakening. Brady wrote that his dad had dropped out of college to work and eventually support a family. Brady realized he could honor his father by doing well in college. "I made a choice," he wrote, "and that choice was to pursue what my father could never do, and to live my life in the remembrance of his name."

When Kathi read that essay out loud, she noticed Andreas Dukas, the cross-country runner who wanted to be an engineer, listening intently, as if it touched on his own life. She didn't say anything to him, though.

One of the most haunting pieces in Essay Writing for College had been written by Chelsea's sister, Annie, a year earlier. She described going through chemotherapy when she was younger, and wearing a wig in a sixth-grade class photo. She said it was her favorite wig and yet she still despised it.

Surprisingly, Annie turned the experience into a hopeful essay. She ended by saying she emerged from her last treatment able to appreciate the world in a new way. She felt like she'd been reborn.

As was often the case with such personal essays, Annie had never before talked in school about her ordeal. She hadn't even revealed that she'd been gravely ill, and Smitty was taken aback when he read the essay.

He hadn't known. He called Annie into his office and asked her to close the door.

"I hope I can say this to you," Smitty said in a gentle voice. "Don't you know that throughout your school career, teachers complained about your absenteeism?"

She nodded.

"You were dealing with cancer?"

Yes, she had been.

To Smitty, both Brady's and Annie's essays had helped them come to terms with issues they might not otherwise have faced.

S mitty never mentioned Annie's essay to her sister, Chelsea. But he later saw Chelsea touch on the same theme.

For one application, Chelsea had to write about a time in her life when she was transformed. She finished it and left a printout in Smitty's office without a comment. It started with an allusion to Nabokov, who described life this way: "A brief crack of light between two eternities of darkness."

By the third sentence, Smitty understood where Chelsea was going. It was about her big sister's illness. Smitty was so moved that he needed to share it with someone. When a young English teacher happened by his office, Smitty said he had to hear this. He began to read it aloud:

It was the morning of our fourth-grade field trip to the Bronx Zoo when my father cradled me like an infant. His eyes went red and watery, and he told me, "Annie has cancer."

At first, I thought his eyes were sweating. I thought his voice was cracking because he was tired. I made up excuses to rationalize the simple act of crying.

I wonder now who it was that told me that crying is a form of weakness. In retrospect, it is probably the strongest I have ever seen my father.

After the last line, both men let a brief silence fall. Smitty spoke first. "What a family," he said.

Each of Kathi's Essay Writing classes had its own distinct feel. The first period was subdued, with Jeff slinking in late, Lee halfheartedly working, and Chelsea with iPod earbuds on in front of a computer, engrossed in reggae, jazz, and pop selections she called the "Get Shit Done" mix.

The other extreme was eighth period. Kathi called it "rambunctious"; Smitty called it "hyper." Kasper often had everyone in eighth period laughing with his stories. One typical afternoon, he told his classmates about going on college visits with his older brother.

"At Brown, I raised my hand in front of the tour guide and I was like, 'This is the *Ivy* League? That's impossible 'cause this place is too chill!' I thought my brother was going to have a heart attack!"

Smitty was glad to have Kasper ease the stress. No one knew what he'd come up with next. One day Kasper and a friend searched Google Earth for a satellite image of the house where Smitty and Kathi lived.

"There it is!" Kasper shouted. "There's Ms. Reilly's black Jeep!" He turned around and declared, "Riles, we found your house!"

Although Smitty did not push Kasper to write about losing his dad because it was too recent, he did think it was an important detail for a college to know. Smitty would mention it in his letter of recommendation.

Kasper's opposite in the class was Andreas Dukas, the silent cross-country runner. He was one of Oyster Bay's mystery kids. Andreas hung out with a lone friend in the back of room 207, cracking jokes and rarely working on his essays. Like Riana, he went through the day doing his best not to attract teachers' attention. But unlike her, he wasn't a standout in any student groups. He was on the margins of school life. His family was, too. His parents owned an ice cream store, and rarely showed up at school events. Andreas was the one kid who'd gone through most of high school without a cell phone. He didn't need it because he had no one to call.

In elementary school, Andreas had been one of Oyster Bay's most promising students. He was moved into accelerated classes. Then, when he was in sixth grade, his older brother, an eleventh grader, died in a car crash. The brothers had been very close, and when Andreas heard the news, he threw plates around the kitchen and punched holes in the walls. He quit the accelerated program and was so sullen in middle school that he was often sent to lunchroom detention. He was sometimes joined there by Jeff Sanders, who had aggravated several teachers in middle school.

Andreas was struck by something Jeff had once said: "I'm really a smart kid, you know. I'm smarter than a lot of people here who think they're smarter than me." Andreas felt the same way. But otherwise, the two were hardly alike. Jeff was a school presence as a jock, while Andreas was mostly invisible.

As a junior, Andreas found a class he loved—physics. And he found a student there he could relate to—Riana. She and Andreas were lab partners, and they shared a curiosity about how things worked. They tried to figure out what was out there after the last galaxy.

He once got caught helping others cheat on a physics test. Instead of just coming down on him, the teacher suggested he was trying to be accepted by the cool kids. Andreas denied it, but Riana knew the teacher was absolutely right.

In Smitty's view, the faculty had failed to appreciate Andreas. Perhaps it was because his grades ranked him 27th out of his class of 109. Then came the first SAT tests during junior year. Smitty was stunned by the results. Andreas had the second highest score of anyone in the class, and he hadn't studied. His combined math and verbal were 1450, second only to Colin's 1460. Andreas edged out the next best, 1410. Lee Kim and Nathaniel had tied with that, and they'd both taken SAT prep courses.

Every year, Smitty had to identify a few seniors who would be Oyster Bay's choices for a New York State academic scholarship, which awarded up to fifteen hundred dollars annually. To sift out candidates, he applied a complex formula based on various state test scores. Jenna, the salutatorian, came in first, which was predictable. But in second place, Andreas had tied Layla, the valedictorian, who often stayed at school working till eleven o'clock. Smitty wondered: How much more might this boy have achieved if someone at Oyster Bay High had encouraged him?

For his first attempt at a college application essay, Andreas wrote about running track. He used words like *bonding* and described his "special and unique" teammates. Writing it was as easy as making up a story, and that's what he'd done. He barely talked to his teammates.

Kathi couldn't tell if the essay was real or false, but she knew it was boilerplate stuff. "Generic," she remarked.

She asked him to find another subject. The admissions office wanted to know who Andreas really was.

Andreas said he could perhaps write about something that happened to his brother. He didn't realize that Kathi knew about the crash. She'd even gone to the memorial service because she'd known the other boy who was killed. Kathi told Andreas that writing about his brother sounded like a good idea.

Andreas reminded Kathi of her own rule: The class was supposed to avoid "pity me" essays.

"Mine is sad," he said. "It might sound like I'm asking for sympathy."

"If you write it the right way," Kathi said, "it will show you learned from something that's sad."

Smitty wondered how Andreas would manage to do a piece about a tragedy he had never talked about. He mentioned it to Matt Brown.

"Just be patient," Matt told Smitty. Matt thought the essay might lead Andreas to open up more in general. He'd already seen progress when Riana persuaded Andreas to go to a SADD meeting. He ended up sitting there quietly, but at least he showed up. The essay topic showed more willingness by Andreas to reveal himself.

There are always kids in high school who are unseen, Matt thought, and people often dismiss them as dull or disinterested. Andreas was proof to him that such kids have hidden depth and gifts. The challenge for a school was to figure out how to tap into that. Perhaps with Andreas Dukas, the college hunt, with its need to offer a self-portrait, would help.

Not all the essays were weighty. One day when Smitty was talking with Jeff and Jenna, Jenna mentioned Barnard's question about a book that influenced her. She'd written about *Harold and the Purple Crayon*.

Jeff gave her a curious look.

"It's a children's book," she said.

Smitty figured admissions officers would be more impressed if Jenna wrote about, say, a novel by Thomas Pynchon, who had graduated from Oyster Bay High. Yet on reflection, Smitty felt she might be onto something. Her outstanding grades showed her academic strength. Her main essay was a poignant remembrance of the day relatives told her uncle, who had Down syndrome, that his mother had died. She wrote that her uncle inspired her to want to do medical research.

Perhaps, thought Smitty, this second piece, on Harold and his crayon, would add levity to her package.

A few years earlier, Oyster Bay's valedictorian was a studious Asian girl named Maya. Unexpectedly, she had written an application essay about, of all things, her infatuation with a boy. She was applying to MIT and Brown. Maya's father came in to tell Smitty he was worried that the topic was too light. But Smitty was delighted by it. He liked the casual tone:

> I giggled as I passed a note to my best friend, Karla. She looked up at the teacher, scribbled some words down, and then passed it back. I opened it carefully, and smiled. "Reid was looking at you before," it read. "He surely likes you back." Drawn all over my papers in big loopy handwriting were the words, "I love Reid."

Smitty felt Maya's scores and recommendations would tell MIT and Brown all they needed to know about her intellect. Her essay humanized her in a way that admissions officers, especially at MIT, seldom saw. "I thought that essay helped her break out of the stereotype that Asian kids are tunnel-visioned academic machines," Smitty recalled.

He knew that during long folder reading sessions at colleges, admissions officers' eyes glaze over. A whimsical essay could make an applicant stand out.

He liked to tell everyone the outcome: Not only did Maya get into MIT and Brown, her piece was included in *Writing an Outstanding College Application Essay*.

By the end of October, the kids in the essay class were getting to some compelling truths. One of the twin girls wrote about her fear of losing her mother years before, after her mom was diagnosed with cancer. The girl remembered worrying that her father lacked enough of a "maternal instinct" to fill both roles.

One day she woke up with a fever, and saw another side of him:

> My dad removed the hair that was stuck to my sweaty face. He then stroked my cheek. There was nothing significant about the gesture. It was simply my father stroking my face. But at that moment, I knew that my father would mold himself to fill those gaps my mother might leave someday.
>
> I knew that he would never fill some gaps, but he'd keep trying.
>
> I knew we would all be okay.

Again, Smitty felt an admissions essay had helped a student see her own life more clearly.

Andreas continued on with his essay about his brother. He was usually a fast writer, but now sat at the computer finishing about one paragraph before it was time to leave room 207 each day. He didn't joke around with his lone friend in the class. He just sat in the back staring at the screen, occasionally tapping out a word or two.

At last, he turned it in. Kathi took the essay home and sat on the couch that night to read it. When she was done, she looked over at Smitty, who lay on his own matching couch. They could hear the wind outside.

"You won't believe this one," Kathi said.

She told him it was Andreas's essay. It opened with his brother, Paul, giving advice: "Don't mess up like me."

Andreas wrote about how he and his parents shut down after Paul's death. It was so painful they stopped mentioning him. Unsettled by the silence at home, Andreas started going to the library. He began to read great authors, starting with Orwell and Twain.

Kathi was impressed with how well he used specific moments to reveal his truths.

> The lives of the characters took on a tangible realness: I felt sympathetic toward their causes, happy when they were happy, sad when they were sad. Literature was the key to a new world, a world other than my own. Anything was better than reality.
>
> I often sneaked into the science section, discreetly browsing Einstein's *Relativity: The Special and General Theory*, or reading up on single-variable calculus. I'm sure I would be quite embarrassed if someone ever walked into my bedroom and saw my stack of quantum mechanics books.

Kathi and Smitty agreed it was one of the best essays produced this fall. The powerful ending showed Andreas was aware of the need to change.

> Some of the old habits still linger, remnants of an internal struggle. I battle with procrastination, and my work ethic needs some attention, but if I have ever made a promise that I intended to keep, it is this one:
> I will not mess up, Paul.

It reminded Smitty of Brady's essay about losing his father and Annie's about her childhood cancer. Smitty was convinced that for all three of these kids, writing the college admissions essay was among their most profound experiences in high school.

FIFTEEN

"My Whole Life Is in That Folder"

Name: Nathaniel Coleman

Weighted GPA: 98.5—25th in the class of 109

SAT: 660 critical reading + 750 math = composite 1410

ACT: N/A

Before the first-period bell sounded on the last Thursday in October, a woman called the guidance office to say that her son, Nathaniel Coleman, was arriving in a few minutes. He needed help with his early application to Columbia.

Nathaniel's counselor, Deanna, smiled at the thought of a mom calling simply to inform her that her child was on his way in. Deanna had heard from Nathaniel's mother often in the last few weeks. She was very involved in the process.

"Mrs. Coleman," Deanna said cheerily, "you can't follow him around at college next year."

Nathaniel was a likable kid who admitted he was confused by the college hunt. He wanted to be an engineer. His mother was an artist and dancer who was now devoting much of her time to helping Nathaniel with his search. She had organized his application materials in bins, highlighted deadlines on a wall calendar, and read many college guidebooks. She'd drawn up a ranking of the top fifty engineering schools, chosen five, then had Nathaniel choose another five. That's how he'd come up with his list.

At first the mom seemed disappointed when Nathaniel didn't get Smitty as his counselor. Deanna, who looked as young as an undergraduate student, had to convince her that she knew plenty about admissions. She'd earned a master's degree in counseling at Fordham. She pointed out that she worked in the office next to Smitty's and sought his counsel when she needed it.

When Nathaniel showed up in the office that Thursday, his long wavy hair was unkempt, his T-shirt was wrinkled, and he seemed on edge. It was Halloween, but he wasn't in the mood to wear a costume.

On a recent visit to Columbia, Nathaniel had missed the tour—and he was glad because the campus guides always sounded like car salesmen. He and his parents checked out the engineering building, and found students designing a biomechanical snake that doctors could insert into a patient's throat to perform surgery. That excited Nathaniel. Up until then, he'd thought about college just in terms of classes. Now he realized he could do his own research.

Nathaniel was known as one of the most formidable math students at Oyster Bay. His 1410 on the SAT was tied with Lee for third best in the senior class, but it was still a bit low for Columbia.

Nathaniel had always built things, first with Legos and then with any available materials. He could look at a model and figure out how to assemble it without instructions. He took trombone and piano lessons, then taught himself to play the guitar. He taught himself to write music, too. He didn't tell others about that. "I do it for myself, not for anyone else," he would say.

He did do some things to impress colleges, though. He'd been on a crew team for years and he was tired of it. He wanted to quit as senior year started, but thought it would look bad to an admissions officer, so he stayed with it. He was on the math team, too. "But that was more or less a résumé filler," he acknowledged.

Deanna found Nathaniel endearing. He could do a complex math problem in seconds, yet he lost his college materials in the black hole of his backpack. He excelled in Oyster Bay's most advanced computer course, yet didn't have a flash drive because it had gone through the washing machine in his pants pocket months before. He could talk about nanotechnology, yet regarded the clock in the guidance office with a mystified look. He explained that he was used to digital displays, and couldn't tell time in analog.

In short, he had a mathematical mind but an absentminded manner. His Columbia app was almost due and he still hadn't finished his résumé or essays. He worked on them, but distractedly, while listening to a symphony on his iPod, waving his hand in the air like a conductor.

"That's Nathaniel," Deanna would say. "You gotta love him."

On this Halloween day, Oyster Bay's younger students walked through the halls as nerds or cats or Captain Underpants. Some of the older kids dressed up, too. In first-period Essay Writing class, Dominique, dressed as a devil, arm-wrestled Chelsea, who wore an angel costume.

Quite a few of the seniors had decided they were above it, though. Or perhaps this was the first year their attention had to be on something else. They seemed to be wondering about the same things: Tomorrow was November. How could they get everything done?

The greatest stress was on those with early-app deadlines, but many adults in the school felt its effects as well. In the second-floor photocopy room, faculty talked about having to do recommendations. Kathi, often voted the senior class's favorite teacher, had been asked to write fifteen so far. A popular history instructor had been asked to do twenty-five.

Downstairs, Smitty was feeling grumpy. He had an ear infection, and the medicine he'd taken had made him feel queasy. He'd made things worse by catching a cold while working at Jeff's football games in chilly stadiums. And today his computer froze just when he was helping a student finish a Common Application. In frustration, Smitty mock-threatened to hit the screen with his shoe.

He often felt tension about now. A few years before, during this same stressful early-app rush, Smitty had stopped by Kathi's class to make an announcement about admissions business. In front of the students, she made it clear that this was her AP English course, not Essay Writing for College. The students watched the testy exchange.

"Uh-oh," one of the girls said, to laughter. "There's trouble in paradise."

Recalling the episode, Smitty chuckled. Then, mindful of his current deadline, he repeated the phrase. "Trouble in paradise."

Nathaniel had put his résumé in a spreadsheet. Deanna sat down to refine it, and soon needed help from Gerard, a grad school guidance intern. The spreadsheet had nearly a dozen typefaces and sizes. It had to be redone completely. They were right up against Columbia's early decision closing date.

As Nathaniel looked on, Gerard made him a new résumé. He typed Nathaniel's activities, starting with jazz band and wind ensemble. He corrected several spelling mistakes. It took him a minute to decipher some of Nathaniel's lines. He puzzled over "Calc III @ NYIT." Then he changed it to "New York Institute of Technology: Currently enrolled in Multivariable Calculus class."

Gerard asked what honors he had earned. Nathaniel said he didn't have many.

"Did you make honor roll?"

"Every quarter," Nathaniel said.

Honor roll, Gerard said deadpan, qualified as an honor. He tried a joke to lighten Nathaniel's mood: "Does the honor roll come with tuna or shrimp?" Nathaniel didn't laugh.

Somehow as Nathaniel got pointers from his counselor and the intern on this October 31, he thought he heard that Columbia's applications were due before November 1. That meant he needed to hit the SUBMIT button by midnight—ten hours away. Actually, the app was due *on* November 1, the end of the following day.

From his office, Smitty watched Gerard and Nathaniel work. Columbia's site said that 93 percent of accepted students were in the top ten of their class. Nathaniel wasn't. Despite his very good SAT score, Nathaniel had a 98.5 average, which would have ranked him twenty-fifth.

"Columbia?" Smitty asked in his office, out of Nathaniel's earshot. He wasn't optimistic.

Last year Penn had accepted a girl who had ranked twenty-fourth, but she had an exceptional story. Her father had worn out his only pair of shoes while working a cattle ranch during his youth in Paraguay. Smitty heard kids complain about the unfairness of such affirmative action, but he didn't feel sorry for them. The ones who protested the loudest didn't realize how many benefits they got out of family connections and money.

Over the next seven hours, the school day flew by while Nathaniel tweaked his essay. Meanwhile, Gerard put the résumé and the sealed recommendations in a folder on the desk of Blossom, the guidance secretary.

As Nathaniel headed out of the guidance cave, he stopped to gaze at the file. It said his name, and then the destination: "Columbia."

"My whole life is in that folder," he said.

The next afternoon, Smitty sat back in his swivel chair and enjoyed the relative peace. The first round was all but over. About 40 percent of the seniors were applying to college through rolling or early applications. That was much lower than the top high schools in the country, where 70 percent or more applied early, in part because higher-income families with college-educated parents tend to prepare for these choices for years. Smitty didn't push early apps too hard. He told his kids that college was too important a decision to rush because of tactics or anxiety. He worried that kids would get a binding acceptance, then later change their minds and feel trapped.

Still, they'd reached a big milestone in the process. The first apps were ready to be delivered, mostly via the Web. Three students were applying to Columbia, making it this year's favorite private college for early apps. Despite the rep's claim that kids from the same school don't compete with one another, Smitty doubted Columbia would fill three of its five hundred freshman slots from Oyster Bay.

Whenever a wave of applications went out, Smitty was left with nagging concerns. A few years before, he was able to proofread any paperwork that went out from his office, but now many students sent apps electronically from home. He worried that kids had misspelled something or given colleges inappropriate e-mail addresses. He'd seen too many addresses like "sexybabe1989" or "beachbum00," which didn't make a good first impression on an admissions officer.

Dominique had finished several applications for drama programs. She had told Kathi her essays were perfect.

"No one needs to look at them," she'd insisted.

Kathi passed that on to Smitty, who decided to proof the printouts anyway. As he read Dominique's essays for Emory, he found five typos. He started to track her down, hoping she hadn't pressed SUBMIT yet.

Outside his door, the guidance office was quiet. Blossom sealed Jenna's early application for Barnard, and Kasper's for both Berkeley and NYU's Stern School of Business.

Nathaniel bounded in to tell Deanna he'd just barely beaten the deadline the night before. At 11:58 P.M., with the seconds ticking down, he'd noticed he had the option of sending a picture, so he raced to find one, crop it, and attach it. He tapped the SUBMIT button at exactly 11:59:22. He'd made it by 38 seconds.

In fact, because of the misunderstanding, Nathaniel finished with 24 hours and 38 seconds to spare. Deanna figured it was just as well.

One more time, Smitty checked over a final few applications. He knew the students felt he overthought things and quite a few even saw him as a control freak. But when tempted to agree, he would glance at the photo of the girl who'd been rejected everywhere.

The last week, as usual, had been a rush. It had also been an enormous amount of work. And it occurred to him that the process had barely begun.

SIXTEEN

Accepted

Allyson Frankel was having a bad day. She'd taken time from school to do errands and was on a train heading home from Manhattan. She was stressed-out, knowing she needed to finish her last applications. More important, Michigan's rolling response was due anytime, and she'd been constantly checking her e-mail for it. She needed to get home to look again.

Suddenly, the train lurched to a stop. Of all unlikely things, it had hit a car. Passengers screamed and the lights went out. With sirens howling all around, the train was evacuated and everyone had to figure out other ways to get home. It was a freezing day—Thursday, November 8—and Allyson was standing outside shivering, waiting for a ride from her father. That wasn't working out well, either; he was stuck in traffic.

It took hours to finally get back to her house in Oyster Bay. Allyson was cold and drained, and she'd all but forgotten the thought that had obsessed her for days.

Then she remembered: Was she in? She went up to her room to check her e-mail.

Nothing. No news from Michigan.

Then, just to be sure, she searched through the items that looked like spam.

And there it was.

The subject line clearly stated it: "University of Michigan Admissions Decision."

At first, she wondered if this was a prank. But it was too official. It was the real thing.

As she opened the message, she saw a blue word: "Congratulations!"

Michigan added some whimsy to their e-mailed acceptances. This one came with an audio flourish. As she opened it, there was the sound of horns, and a band began playing. It made her smile. Then she opened a video greeting from a professor saying, "I want to be the first to welcome you."

Allyson screamed the news to her parents downstairs. She started crying. She grabbed her cell to call her boyfriend in Philadelphia.

It was the first acceptance for the Oyster Bay High senior class of 2008. Allyson Frankel was into a college, and her top choice, no less.

She was relieved, of course, and thrilled, but she also had an unexpected emotion. She knew about senior slump, the malaise that sets in once you're accepted and have less motivation to keep doing schoolwork. With Allyson, it was the opposite. She felt newly energized about the next seven months. She realized that too much of high school, especially the last year, had been a stressful race to deliver for college. Now that she had done so, at last, she could actually enjoy her classes for their own sake.

Smitty nagged students to finish their work early, but he didn't follow his own advice. He put off writing recommendations as long as he could, though mostly for pragmatic reasons. He liked to first read final essays and see the latest scores.

It was an irony, he thought, that although the college hunt is all about senior year, by default, kids have to sell themselves on what they did earlier. But Smitty knew this first semester of senior year brought plenty of new achievements, and he wanted admissions folks to appreciate those, too. That's why he asked his friend Matt, the social worker, to update him on Riana Tyson's projects at SADD.

Smitty felt the best teachers offered the best insights. Karen Crowley, an art teacher, had a classroom across the hall from the guidance suite, and, like Smitty, often worked into the night. Karen advised the literary magazine, and one evening she stopped by Smitty's office to share some thoughts about Lee Kim, who was the magazine's editor.

Karen knew that some regarded Lee as standoffish, but she saw another side. Lee spent hours polishing students' submissions, and even organized a pizza party to encourage younger kids to join the staff. "He puts his heart and soul into making the magazine a success," Karen said.

Another time, Karen told Smitty about one of her star students, Chelsea Flynn. Chelsea had taken a series of pictures of a boy who had a tumor removed, and Karen described the poignant images of scars on the boy's back. Karen thought that something—maybe the experience with her sister's illness—had made Chelsea especially compassionate.

Karen laughed as she described the night Chelsea had come in for help putting together a photo portfolio for colleges. Chelsea had done it at the last minute, of course. "Chelsea definitely has an artistic temperament, but she's not a narcissist or egotistic," Karen said. "People love her."

It was Karen who pointed out the similarity between Chelsea and Jeff Sanders. Karen worked as a timekeeper at basketball games, and she told Smitty how impressed she was with Jeff's graceful moves on the court and his intense focus. During a game, he seemed to know where every one of his teammates and opponents were at all moments. "In the gym, Jeff has the kind of intensity that Chelsea has in the studio."

Another of Smitty's favorite teachers, Matthew Sisia, the band director, said he'd been surprised by Jeff. The boy continued to play the tuba senior year, long after many kids decided band wasn't cool. Although Jeff wasn't a great musician, he persevered.

"You look at Jeff and at first he seems like a slacker," Matthew told Smitty. "But a slacker would've dropped music and taken a free period."

Sometimes the most telling details came unexpectedly. One day, Smitty was wrapping up a meeting with Dominique and her mother. "I never buy her clothes," her mom happened to say as they put on their coats. "She designs and sews them herself." That wasn't typical for a girl in the New York suburbs, and it gave Smitty one more detail to help emphasize Dominique's creativity when describing her to theater schools.

When he at last sat down to write a recommendation, Smitty sought to follow the same rules he and Kathi gave to students. He tried to use specifics, keep himself to a single page, and tell it like a story, from beginning to end.

He was now in the thick of his own essay writing.

Often, a counselor's recommendation could reveal what kids couldn't about themselves. One of Smitty's most interesting students was Curtis, who had an A average, was president of the senior class, and played on the varsity tennis team. Impressive, but on the surface, admissions people at top schools might see him as a typical well-rounded student. Every high school produced plenty of these applicants. Smitty's letter was a way to show how different Curtis was: He still faced operations from childhood meningitis, and his dad had left the family.

Kathi, also doing a recommendation for Curtis, had written hers first. She explained that Curtis's mother had been forced to sell her house and move to an apartment, at which time Curtis's "very comfortable" lifestyle ended. "And yet as a student in my honors English class," she wrote, "he never allowed his personal life to interfere with his work ethic."

Smitty picked up the theme in his own letter. "I cannot fathom the ordeals with which he has had to cope, and, more impressively, few know of these circumstances." He continued:

> I was astounded that his performance remained unchanged, his personality remained upbeat, and he never lost that wonderful sense of humor. He simply stated that he needed to take care of his mother. Her life was shattered, and he was the only person who could help. And he was fifteen years old!

When Smitty read Curtis's own essay, he was surprised at a key detail. Curtis wrote of his admiration for his dad. Nowhere did he mention that his father had abandoned the family.

Smitty called him into the guidance office. "Let me understand this: I wrote that your father left and you wrote that he's a great father. Which is accurate?" Smitty said he'd be happy to change his version.

Curtis avoided Smitty's eyes. "What you wrote is true, Mr. Smith."

The exchange prompted Curtis to go back and rework his essay. In a couple of days he turned out a new one. He started by recalling the day Kathi read the opening of *The Catcher in the Rye* to his class, where Holden Caulfield says the reader will probably want to know "where I was born, and what my lousy childhood was like . . . and all that David Copperfield kind of crap."

Curtis wrote of Holden, "I did want to know where he was born, about his lousy childhood, and that David Copperfield kind of crap." Indeed, Holden Caulfield's struggles made him think about his own life.

> I found a connection to Holden. It is not that I did not want to grow up; I am more than ready. It is not that I alienated myself. I am more than willing to interact with people. I did not break down and become lonely and hate the world.
>
> Instead, I took nothing for granted, cherished what I had, and used my friends and my daily activities as motivation to move forward.

Smitty and Kathi usually discouraged essays about *Catcher* because so many kids have written about it since it was published in 1951, but in this case it seemed appropriate. It helped Curtis get to his truth.

Between that essay and the recommendations he'd gathered from Oyster Bay teachers, Curtis was done. Smitty sent out a packet to his first-choice school, the University of Miami.

Shortly after nine A.M. on Friday, November 9, Kathi tried to get the seniors in her AP English class to talk about something other than college. Today, she said, they needed to discuss the fiction of Sandra Cisneros, author of *The House on Mango Street*.

It was a lost cause. The twin boys were discussing Tulane, where they'd both applied. One had been accepted early and the other hadn't heard. Meanwhile, they were mostly anxious about Vanderbilt, which would announce early decisions in a month.

Then Allyson Frankel burst into the classroom.

"I got into Michigan!" she shouted.

Everyone cheered. Allyson described the e-mail she'd gotten the night before—the drumroll, the horns. In her rush to tell about it, she had a brain glitch and said there was even a video welcome message from La Toya Jackson.

Her classmates looked perplexed. Michael Jackson's sister?

"Well, maybe not La Toya," said Allyson, "but it was Professor Jackson or somebody."

Everyone gave Allyson another round of applause.

As the class continued, things got more somber. The others realized how much longer they had to wait for their own news. "I'm not going to know until December," said Kasper, who'd just sent out his Berkeley, Binghamton, and NYU applications.

"I'm not going to know until *April*," said Layla.

Kathi asked everyone to calm down.

"Calm down?" said Kasper. "It's only the next four years of our lives!"

Allyson, still on a high, rushed downstairs to tell Smitty. For this class, it was the first triumph. Allyson had done everything right—written good essays, met deadlines, stayed organized, and gotten into her top choice.

The school had a tradition of hanging a hand-lettered pennant on the wall outside the guidance suite when a student committed to a college. Now Blossom, the secretary, wrote, "Allyson Frankel, University of Michigan" in cursive on a small banner and put it above the doors.

Smitty admired it as he walked out of the office.

One down, 108 to go.

SEVENTEEN

Shopping for Riana

A cold rain fell as Smitty and Kathi emerged from the subway at Broadway and 116th Street—the entrance to Columbia University. The wind whipped Kathi's umbrella, which was decorated with the names of Steinbeck, Plath, and other authors. The two were acting as tour guides today.

They had brought a small group of Oyster Bay teachers and counselors to visit four campuses in Manhattan and the Bronx. Some didn't come into the city much. One of the women cleaned her hands with a disinfectant wipe as they walked out of the subway.

They began a tour of Columbia with a Barnard student who had graduated from Oyster Bay in June. Deanna, the counselor, asked about her schedule. The young woman spoke about biomedical engineering classes, labs, an internship, and her plans for a summer job.

Smitty laughed. "It's November of your freshman year, my dear. Take a breath." But that, he told himself, was Barnard, and he filed the thought away. Students eager to immerse themselves in a hundred activities would likely fit in well here.

As the group strolled past the Butler Library, Smitty paused to look at the façade engraved with the names of Homer, Sophocles, and Aristotle.

"I love this campus," he said.

Part of Smitty's mission was to show his colleagues they could be comfortable recommending urban schools. Many suburban parents feared enrolling their kids in the big, unsafe city. But such qualms were often unfounded. Smitty knew urban campuses could be serene islands, and as for security, the worst recent cases of campus violence involved schools far from urban areas. In the spring, a Virginia Tech student killed thirty-two people and then himself. Later, a Delaware State freshman shot and wounded two students. And a freshman at the University of Arizona was charged with stabbing her roommate to death.

Another reason for Smitty's visit this day was that Oyster Bay kids had become more interested in urban schools as memories of 9/11 faded. Nathaniel and two other kids had applied early to Columbia. Layla and Jenna, the valedictorian and the salutatorian, were trying for all-female Barnard, which Smitty saw as a good strategy. The odds of getting into a women's college were better.

Smitty hoped that some of his early applicants would get good news soon. They needed a break. Even Jenna, who had helped Jeff get organized, seemed to be flagging after months of writing apps. Parents often assumed that kids could cover their whole list by filling out the Common Application, but most colleges asked for a slew of additional forms, essays, and small compositions.

Jenna found that schools like Barnard, Brown, and Salve Regina in Rhode Island required a short essay about why a student was interested in attending. Like many kids, she found a shortcut. She wrote one master composition and tailored it slightly. Her essay for Barnard opened with someone bursting through the door and tapping Jenna on the shoulder, saying, "I'm going to Barnard."

In the Brown essay the person said, "I'm going to Brown."

In the Salve Regina essay the person said, "I'm going to Salve Regina."

The group's next stop was the City College of New York at the northern edge of Harlem, a quick subway ride from Columbia. Smitty knew the campus would surprise most of his colleagues. They entered a grassy quad—a green courtyard in City College, of all places. It swept up to a gracious stone building with two towers rising from a slate roof. Smitty pointed to the hundreds of grotesques, the gargoyle-like figures adorning the building's sides. That was the second surprise—the Gothic architecture.

"It's so campusy," one of the young counselors enthused.

Smitty knew they would now have a new view of the school, and perhaps be more likely to tell kids to consider it.

He said City College had been known as the "Harvard of the Proletariat"—a place where the less privileged could find an exceptional education. Its alumni included Dr. Jonas Salk and Colin Powell. A commuter school for most of its 160 years, it had recently opened a six-hundred-bed dormitory—an assurance to families that might fear "City" would have few housing options. Smitty's favorite feature in the new dorm was in the laundry room, where washers and dryers had a piece of technology geared for this generation. The machines sent text messages to students telling them when their clothes were ready. Smitty wondered: Could the washing machines of Ivy League schools do that?

The group sat with the school's admissions director in a conference

room. He said City offered more than a hundred majors, from biomedicine
to visual arts. The director mentioned another big selling point: Tuition at
City was four thousand dollars a year for New York residents.

Knowing the tight budgets of many families, Smitty had been building
a list of low-cost schools; this would now rank high on it. As everyone took
in the mention of the affordable tuition, Smitty said, to no one in particular, "Riana."

It wasn't the only thing that made him think of her. City College had
an online application with no essays. That would be a bonus for Riana,
who hadn't finished hers yet. And he knew that with her mix of friends,
she'd like the school's diversity: He'd spotted a bulletin board with a sign
announcing a food sale by the Ghanaian students' association.

Riana had recently stopped by his office looking somber. "Mr. Smith,
there's a problem," she said. "I want to study about thirty things at the
same time." He'd laughed at the time, but now he could tell her that she
could come close to that at City.

The group moved on to a student tour. The guide described the exceptional aid package of the new honors program that made him choose City
over other picks. He was offered free tuition, a notebook computer, an
academic expense account that covered study abroad, and a pass for entry
to New York museums.

It made one of the guidance counselors think of another Oyster Bay
student.

"Evan," the counselor whispered.

That was Nathaniel Coleman's best friend, an easygoing kid with
divorced parents and a younger sister who would also soon be going to
college. Two tuitions for one family living in two houses. Others nodded.
Given what they'd been hearing, and given the times, the Harvard of the
Proletariat could well emerge as a magnet for Oyster Bay students.

. . .

The group moved on to Fordham, another school in a borough with an urban jungle image. Instead, they found an unexpectedly peaceful campus. "With all this open space," Smitty observed, "you wouldn't know you were in the Bronx."

At the admissions office, Smitty warmly greeted a man with large glasses, the assistant vice president for enrollment. They'd last seen each other at the Austin conference in September, when Smitty talked up Jeff Sanders. The VP said he remembered their talk about Jeff, and hoped to still see progress. This would be Smitty's last chance to make Jeff's case in person. He felt he needed to be honest.

"He's working on those grades," he said, "but, candidly, I haven't seen the improvements we'd hoped for." Smitty offered an explanation. "The house is filled with relatives the family has taken in. We counted fourteen."

And yet Smitty was mindful that it's no victory to talk a student into a school that might be too challenging. He knew Fordham liked students with a GPA of at least 93, and Jeff was a long way from that, with an unpromising performance in the first weeks of the quarter.

Jeff might still pull himself up, but so far he wasn't ready for Fordham. At this point, Smitty wasn't convinced it was the right fit for other reasons. Jeff was a casual boy, and he might feel constrained at Fordham, a Jesuit school.

As their campus tour continued, Smitty thought about his priorities as a guidance counselor. He reminded himself it was too simple to measure success by prestige acceptances. The true measure would be whether they turned out to be the right places.

In many cases, Smitty knew, he'd have to wait four years to truly know how well he had done with this class.

Soon, the group was on its way out of the city and back home.

EIGHTEEN

"I'm Kicking It Up"

The day after touring the New York campuses, Smitty met at the round table in his office with Jeff and his girlfriend, Jenna. Smitty rarely had couples come in together for an advising session, but given Jeff's grades, he felt he could use an assist.

He thanked Jenna for her help in organizing Jeff's admission files.

"This woman is a keeper," he told Jeff. "Don't screw this up."

Then Smitty got down to business. He needed to put a school on Jeff's radar that was more realistic than Fordham. He told Jeff to consider the City College of New York. "Absolute gem," Smitty said, and then he described the Gothic buildings surrounding a green and the new six-hundred-bed dorm.

Jeff asked what kind of athletics they had.

Smitty said they were Division III, with a decent basketball team, the Beavers. Jeff looked unenthusiastic. Smitty knew what was on his mind: Why the sudden focus on City instead of Fordham?

Smitty decided to be blunt. "I talked to the Fordham vice president when I was on campus yesterday," he said. "He knows about you. Said he's got to see some evidence."

Jeff took this in silently. His foot moved back and forth.

Smitty continued. "Candidly," he said, "your first-quarter progress report sucked."

He recited three of the grades from memory: 50 in precalculus, 70 in physics, 72 in Spanish. "Those are not the kind of numbers you want going to colleges."

Jeff nodded. He knew that. But he was good under pressure, and he'd improved in those classes since the midterm reports. "Not to sound cocky," he said, "but I'm capable of better work. I'm kicking it up."

Smitty reminded Jeff that he'd seemed just as confident months before when he wanted to apply early to Fordham. "They would've said to me, 'Smitty, give me Jeff's first-quarter report,' and that would have killed your chances."

It was Jeff's turn to make a case. He said he was about to take an EMT test in a few days, and then he'd have nights free to do homework.

Smitty took on a fatherly tone. "You've got so many things going for you. You're smart, you're responsible, an excellent athlete with a great character." He added that Jeff had a story to tell to colleges. But there wasn't much time left. Jeff needed to ramp up his grades in the next quarter.

"If you don't have that, then you're dead. I cannot tell you strongly enough."

He brought up Jeff's situation at home.

"You have got to find a quiet place, a place you can get some solitude in the craziness of your home, and I don't mean that in a disparaging way."

Jenna made a suggestion. "School is open at night," she pointed out. "Layla studies here." Smitty liked the idea. He said the janitor locked the building at about eleven o'clock. He knew because he'd spent many nights working till then.

Now he turned his attention to Jenna. She had applied early to Barnard and would hear in a few days. But Jenna wasn't like many early candidates who held off on applying to other schools. In case Barnard said no, she had already sent in packages to Columbia, NYU, Brown, Quinnipiac, Fordham, and Fairfield. She planned to do one more, for Salve Regina.

"If I don't get into Barnard," she said, "something else good will come along." It seemed more a question than a statement.

Smitty agreed. "Next year at this time, my dear, you'll be in a good college."

He looked at Jeff. "And you, too, young man."

Most applicants regarded the essay as a burden, just wanting it over with. Chelsea was different. She looked forward to writing hers. She enjoyed playing with words and ideas. Smitty had rarely seen a senior like Chelsea: She wrote an essay for the pure challenge, then threw it out and tried a wholly different topic.

Her latest attempt focused on two worlds she experienced each year: one at Oyster Bay High, the other at a country club where she raced sailboats in the summer. She talked about feeling torn between them. She loved her diverse friends from public school, yet she felt a tug when the kids at the club discussed the intriguing subjects they studied at their boarding schools—like architecture, Russian philosophy, and business.

Smitty liked the way Chelsea used her writing to work through issues she might not have otherwise sorted out. He read the essay over Chelsea's shoulder.

"Love it!" he said. He particularly liked the final sentence.

"College," Chelsea had written, "will answer my questions."

Other kids seemed more interested in typing the exact number of words required, but Chelsea liked thinking about who she was in her writing—just what Smitty hoped these essays would elicit. He felt it showed a maturity that would help her in the admissions process as much as high scores or extracurriculars.

The essay was ready to go, Smitty said.

A few days later, however, Chelsea got rid of it. She wanted to try something else.

College counseling didn't stop after the applications were done. Kasper had sent in his packets, but soon after, he came in to see Smitty. He'd applied early to NYU's Stern School of Business, and sent regular apps to Binghamton and the University of California at Berkeley's Haas School of Business. He would get NYU's decision any day now, and he was nervous.

"I'm intimidated by Layla's applications," he admitted.

He and Layla were good friends, and similar in many ways. Layla was the highest-ranked girl in the class and Kasper was the highest-ranked boy. Their ACT and SAT scores were nearly identical and they were in the same clubs. Layla's mother was from Iran, just like Kasper's parents.

The two did have different religious backgrounds: Kasper was Muslim and Layla was Jewish. And they really parted ways when it came to applying to colleges. Kasper had applied to just three, Layla to twenty-eight—more if you counted seven-year med programs. Kasper said Layla's approach reminded him of the saying "Shoot for the moon and even if you miss you'll land among the stars." He worried his three schools meant he was shooting too low.

"The question isn't how many schools you apply to," Smitty assured him. "It's how you feel about those schools."

Kasper said NYU was his dream college, and he liked Berkeley and Binghamton as well.

That was important, said Smitty. Getting into premier schools was never certain, but Kasper's transcript should at least assure him a spot at Binghamton.

Kasper lingered, chatting about other things, none of them vital, and finally stood to leave. Smitty wished Kasper luck with the NYU decision.

It occurred to Smitty that perhaps Kasper just wanted to talk to an adult. It had been three months since he'd lost his dad in the train accident.

Smitty decided to read Kasper's essay. It was about a person who'd influenced him. He had chosen his father, which surprised Smitty, who'd assumed the loss might have been too fresh to write about. He was glad Kasper had taken it on.

It started with a memory from their final family trip. "Crying, screaming, and laughing were the sounds that flooded my ears as my father navigated through foreign Spain."

Lightheartedly, he went on to describe his own attempts to translate Spanish for his parents as they moved through the country. He recalled the way his dad and he pretended to be talking to each other over two-way radios, complete with imitation static.

It was a sophisticated piece of writing, using sounds as a subtheme, and it built to a powerful ending.

"Silence. No longer will I hear the lessons or even laughter from my father. The words already spoken are the ones that will stay with me forever."

On the morning of December 11, Nathaniel Coleman couldn't concentrate. Columbia's early decisions would be released in the afternoon. He wondered how he would fill the time until he found out. He had liked

Columbia when he'd taken a summer course there. He wanted to be in Manhattan, and he was ready for this whole college chase to be over.

His mom was equally anxious. She had gone so far as to visit a psychic, who said Columbia looked promising. Nathaniel, a math-and-science person, put little stock in such predictions.

When he arrived at his AP government class, he noticed a substitute teacher inside, so he pivoted and went downstairs to relax in the band room. Dropping his backpack, he sat at a black upright piano and started to play "Moon" by George Winston.

He stopped, grew fidgety, then walked into a storage closet, and returned with a trombone and a sheet of music. He set the music on a stand and started in.

After a few minutes, he stopped again. There was one other student in the room. "I'm not really playing well," Nathaniel admitted to her. "I'm just not really focused right now."

He went back to it anyway. He didn't know what else to do with himself.

The sound of his trombone filled the first-floor hallway.

NINETEEN

"Columbia Didn't Reject Me, I Rejected Columbia"

Nathaniel Coleman was an hour from hearing whether Columbia had accepted him. Applicants would be able to learn their verdict on the school Web site at five P.M., when it would be posted in each account. Nathaniel looked at his digital watch during after-school fencing practice in the gymnasium—fifty-nine minutes to go.

"The object is to hit your opponent," the coach said, "not miss."

The other kids laughed. Nathaniel nodded, but was paying little attention. Fifty-eight minutes.

As the coach talked about the ideal distance to stand from your foe, Nathaniel was wondering if he could have done anything differently for Columbia.

He glanced at his watch. Thirty-eight minutes to go. His alum interview at Starbucks had gone well. His SATs were very good. And—not that he really believed it—the psychic had told his mom things looked positive.

Finally, he headed outside, still wearing his white jacket and foil vest.

He took out his iPhone—it was now 4:59 P.M.—and went onto Columbia's site.

A fencing teammate, a tenth-grader named Alexi had walked out with him. She seemed just as tense as he was as he tried to enter his password. He squinted at the iPhone.

"Nothing," he told her, and touched the screen to refresh the site.

For December, it was a surprisingly warm evening.

"Now?" Alexi asked. Still nothing.

At 5:03, a message came in from Columbia University's admissions office. He opened it.

"Dear Nathaniel," it said, "I regret to inform you . . ."

Nathaniel stared for a beat.

"No," he said flatly.

"No?" repeated Alexi. "No news?"

"No, I'm not going to Columbia."

Nathaniel's eyes teared up. Alexi got emotional, too, and hugged him.

She waited a few seconds. "You have a second choice?"

"No. I wanted to go to school in New York City." He hadn't chosen any other schools in the city. "Now I'm gonna be far away."

She tried to catch his eye. She understood this was one of the most profound disappointments that kids in high school face.

"You can come home on weekends," she suggested. She didn't know what else to say. The two of them stood silently for a moment.

Nathaniel wiped his glasses, opened the double doors, and slowly walked back into the gym.

A couple of miles away, in her house, Adati, the daughter of Indian immigrants, received the same message. Nearby, Zara, whose parents were born in Bangladesh, was also told no. It was not a good day for Oyster Bay High's future engineer, surgeon, and lawyer. In the Columbia early decision sweepstakes, Oyster Bay was 0-for-3.

Smitty had gotten an inkling of Columbia's decisions a week in advance. He'd called a contact in the admissions office who told him it was going to be a very competitive year. Smitty took that as code that his kids should start to think of other options.

Some guidance counselors, Smitty knew, lobby hard with phone calls and even berate admissions officers for rejecting a kid. Smitty believed in being cordial. A guidance counselor, he felt, can never know how his applicants stack up against the national competition. You can make your case, but you can't tell colleges how to do their job.

He also believed that rejection is sometimes a blessing. He'd learned this from the experience of his own daughter, Nicole. She was a top student at a rigorous public school, and had an unusual credential: She'd had a speaking part in a movie starring Helen Hunt. At the start of her senior year, she decided she wanted to go to Harvard after hearing friends rave about it. She was disappointed when Harvard deferred her early bid, and upset when they rejected her in the spring.

She ended up at Duke and had all but forgotten Harvard by the time she arrived in Durham. In Nicole's freshman year, she got to know the school's president when she took a course taught by him and served as a student rep on a committee that worked with his office. One day, Nicole told her dad she was going on a picnic with Duke's president and his wife.

"Do you think you'd be having a picnic with Derek Bok?" Smitty said, referring to Harvard's president.

Smitty knew this would be a very bad week for the three kids rebuffed by Columbia. But he was confident they would in time find a place they were meant to be.

A s Nathaniel walked back into the gym, other kids started to ask what Columbia said. He did not have to answer. They could tell by looking at him.

"You'll get into the other schools," one teammate told him.

"They blew it—you're great!" said another.

One of his coaches put her hand on his shoulder. "Try NYU. They have a fencing team."

"Yeah," Nathaniel said, sounding unconvinced.

He lingered in the gym, chatting with the others. He looked at some of the fencing equipment. He had only recently taken up the sport, having put it off to do other activities meant to impress colleges. It struck him that it was time to do more things for himself, and not some admissions person. Twenty minutes after he'd been shot down by his dream college, Nathaniel Coleman was smiling again.

O n that same December 11 night, Smitty worked late in his office and Kathi stayed to grade papers. They came home long after dark, and found the light blinking on the answering machine. Neither was feeling upbeat. Although they'd expected it, the news from Columbia had made for a bad day.

Smitty pushed the button to hear the message. They heard the voice of Adati, the girl who wanted to be a surgeon. She told them she'd been rejected, but she spoke in a surprisingly chipper voice. "I wanted to thank you so, so, so, so, so much for helping me," she said.

She added that she knew she'd get into a school that was better for her. "Columbia didn't reject me, I rejected Columbia," Adati said. "I love you, Ms. Reilly. Love you, Mr. Smith."

Smitty marveled. On this night of rejection, Adati's call told him she had achieved a more important kind of acceptance than any college admissions office could provide.

TWENTY

Kerplunking

Coughing drily, Kasper excused himself from his AP government class to see the nurse. It was 12:10 P.M., about the time the mailman usually arrived. Today, he would likely bring the decision from NYU.

At the nurse's office, Kasper came clean. "I'm not sick," he admitted. "My college letter is in the mail."

The nurse wasn't surprised. It was a busy week for early application decisions. She already had seen several seniors with mysterious illnesses that could be cured only by retrieving a letter or checking e-mail.

In the days since Columbia had rejected Nathaniel, Adati, and Zara, Oyster Bay had received welcome news. Colin, the crew recruit, got into Dartmouth, a notable banner for the wall outside the guidance cave. Other kids had been accepted early to Johnson & Wales, Penn State, and Delaware. It seemed that every few hours another senior was shouting on a cell phone in the stairway. "Mom, I got into Northeastern." "Mom? Mom? Can you hear me?"

The twin girls got into the University of Maryland, one on a full soccer scholarship. In a big triumph, the twin boys got into Vanderbilt. They
showed up at Kathi's classroom in Vanderbilt T-shirts that their grandmother had optimistically ordered. They had reason to celebrate: Vanderbilt had received a record 1,133 early decision applicants, a 41 percent
increase over the previous year.

The nurse winked at Kasper and told him to go home. She wished him
luck with the mail. Kasper had a few friends who had heard from NYU the
day before. The friends lived closer to New York City than he did. Kasper
pictured decision letters coming out of Manhattan in waves. He expected his
own was almost at his door, and meaningfully, on his dad's birthday. He'd get
it, then stop by the cemetery to celebrate or commiserate with his father.

For those who had been rejected, it was a different kind of week. Many,
resigned, resumed the application process. Nathaniel Coleman, in the
wake of his Columbia rejection, was back in Kathi Reilly's class, trying to
work on an essay for Cornell. He wasn't getting far.

She was with another student when Nathaniel asked for help.

She came over and he explained his trouble. "I have to incorporate
myself into it, and I don't know how to do that." He was trying to write a
standard five-hundred-word miniessay on why he wanted to go to Cornell.

Kathi read his first sentence:

"I was interested in becoming an engineer since my early childhood."

She did not sugarcoat her reaction.

"*Blech,*" she said. She struck out the sentence with her red pen.

Kathi knew that students were often stumped by this question. It was
hard to find interesting ways to explain why they liked a school. She asked
for the class's attention, and described Nathaniel's dilemma. The question "Why Cornell?" was deceptive, Kathi told the kids. Too often, it led

applicants to merely recite highlights from the Web site. That's not what an admissions officer wanted. It was better to choose unusual details that revealed as much about yourself as the college.

She told the class about a boy last year who had set his sights on Tufts. He had just fifty words to describe why he liked it. During a visit to campus, he'd observed a class on the Middle East. He'd learned about a Tufts semester-in-Washington program. He'd read about a seminar on Bill Clinton's presidency. Squeezing all that in was tricky.

Kathi read his solution aloud:

Only 50 words?! I'll try—
Opportunity to focus on political science subfields
The Clinton seminar!
Courses are relevant—not too abstract
Friendly, diverse student body
Professor Mufti's class on Middle Eastern relations—sat in, would
    have loved to participate
Great student-teacher ratio
Tufts-in-Washington . . .
To name a few!

"It's like haiku," one of the girls said in appreciation.

"It is creative," Kathi agreed. She asked them to picture a Tufts folder reader finally coming across a punchy approach after a hundred dry ones. The boy was accepted.

Kathi reminded them about the girl who wanted to be in premed at Chicago the year before. Her test scores weren't great, so she needed to do a first-rate essay. Asked to explain her attraction to the school, she'd started by describing Jackson Pollock's style of painting. "He dripped, dropped, splattered, flung, splashed, spurt, sprinkled, and kerplunked, unafraid to venture beyond the periphery of conventionalism." She wrote that the creativity at the University of Chicago reminded her of Jackson Pollock. "I look forward to some serious kerplunking at the University of Chicago," she concluded.

Kerplunking? Smitty and Kathi loved that essay, and they'd heard that Chicago's admissions officers considered it one of the best of the year.

In that vein, Kathi encouraged the students to have fun with their writing. They could draw inspiration from poetry and music. They could experiment with sentence fragments and try to flatter colleges with inspired examples of what makes the school unique. The main rule was to avoid dull, predictable prose.

Nathaniel agreed to give it another try.

Often, the students were stymied by another standard essay—one asking them to describe themselves. Some recited a list of activities while others boasted of an accomplishment. Both approaches were wrong, Kathi said. To describe themselves effectively, Kathi offered four questions to think about:

What makes you different from your friends or siblings?
What experiences have shaped your personality?
What mistakes have you made?
What have you learned from those mistakes?

Kathi and Smitty had several other prompts that helped kids focus. One came from the Tufts application, and it included these questions:

Do you surf?
Are you a vegetarian?

Did you wear flip-flops to the prom?

Do you have a tattoo?

Who are you?

Another two came from Bates College:

What quality do you like best in yourself and what do you like least?

What quality would you most like to see flourish and which would you like to see wither?

Yet another came from Penn:

You have just completed your 300-page autobiography. Please submit page 217.

Smitty liked that last question. It forced kids to think about their future. Would they be working or raising a family by page 217? Retired and playing golf? Kathi had heard the tale—perhaps apocryphal—that one father called Penn's admissions office to ask for an extra couple of weeks for his daughter, since she'd written only up to page 150.

Another college had asked kids to tell them the most daring thing they'd ever done. One boy's answer was to draw a defiant red slash across the essay question and let that stand as the answer.

Whenever Kathi told that last story, kids would ask if the boy got in.

Yes, she replied.

"But," Smitty added, "he was a legacy."

Tufts gave students the option of filling a page any way they wanted. Nathaniel was thinking of doodling on it. Smitty hoped he would avoid that temptation. Nathaniel was not a legacy.

When he got home, Kasper found an envelope with a purple NYU insignia on it. And it was thick. He was in.

He drove to the cemetery and told his father about it. He'd be attending NYU's Stern School of Business, his first choice. Then he raced back to school to share his good news. In the hallway, he ran into Jeff's girlfriend, Jenna. He could tell she was equally excited. She had just heard from Barnard.

"I got in!" cried Jenna—Barnard class of 2012.

"I got in!" cried Kasper—NYU class of 2012.

They'd known each other since childhood. Kasper had comforted Jenna when her grandmother died, and Jenna had comforted Kasper when his father died. Now they'd be just a subway ride away from each other.

Jenna told Kasper more good news: She had gotten a financial aid package that would cover all her expenses.

They headed to the guidance suite. Smitty embraced them. He considered each a terrific story. Kasper, the son of Iranian immigrants, had stayed optimistic after his father's death; Jenna, daughter of a bayman and a nurse, had risen to salutatorian. She'd earned a free ticket to a college considered part of the Ivy League family.

Smitty liked to say that the process mattered more than the results: The highest goal was seeing kids grow emotionally. But he was a pragmatist, too. His work was getting kids into the schools where they wanted to go. There were few things he loved more in this job than when they shared good news.

TWENTY-ONE

"She Would've Been a Slam Dunk"

Name: Layla Eran

Weighted GPA: 108.4—1st in the class of 109

SAT: 680 critical reading + 720 math = 1400 composite

ACT: 32

L ate one night, the school smelled like floor wax, the chairs rested upside down on desks, and everything was still. At this hour, there was just one sound—the echo of a solitary keyboard clicking. Layla Eran, who was sending out twenty-eight applications, was at work.

Layla thought many kids saw her as a stereotype: the valedictorian; the grind; Miss Perfect. She realized she played into that image, with her relentless work ethic, and her black shirts, black boot-cut pants, and black laptop, matching her dark hair. She was the girl kids approached to ask if they could copy homework, and she was the girl who said no.

She had taken eight AP courses by senior year and earned top grades. She'd also gotten a 97 or above in five of New York's Regents exams.

She was just as high-achieving outside the classroom. She had been a student government president and was in SADD, the Gay-Straight Alliance, and a community service club. Outside of school, she volunteered each week at a senior center helping an older woman who had been abandoned by her family. She liked to encourage other kids to get involved, grabbing their attention by saying it would look good for college admission.

Layla appeared to have it easy, but things weren't as they seemed. Her mother was a Jewish woman from Iran who had fled during the Shah's reign. Her father, from New York, was also Jewish. They'd divorced when she was three, and Layla, an only child, lived with her mom, a psychoanalyst. Her mother often worked late, and many nights Layla stayed at school till eleven P.M.

"I should pay rent," she joked.

After Layla's parents split, one person had made a point of offering to help—Kasper's father, a Muslim who shared her Iranian roots. Kasper's dad told Layla's mom if she needed anything at all, she could consider it done. Layla was always touched by that.

As kids, Layla and Kasper were involved in the same activities. They'd both been top students since elementary school. Kasper's dad was a gentle older man who laughed easily. He would ask Layla what grade she'd gotten, and pretended to scold Kasper if he lagged behind. Usually, their grades came out the same. Their SAT scores were almost identical, and he'd gotten 31 on the ACT while she got 32. When Kasper's dad was hit by a train in a summer storm, Layla felt like she'd lost a father, too.

She was there in Essay Writing when Ms. Reilly had read the opening sentences of Kasper's essay. Layla choked up as Ms. Reilly got to the one-word sentence about how Kasper would no longer hear his father's voice: "Silence."

If kids asked about her life, Layla said, they'd understand her drive to do well in school. She had family and friends who drank and did drugs. She had a cousin who had mental-health problems, and the experts who treated him seemed to make him worse. She thought the world needed better professionals. She planned to go to medical school and become a psychiatrist.

For a while, Layla considered applying somewhere early. Lots of Web sites said kids who applied early had far better odds of getting in. But when she thought about that, she found it misleading. Sure, colleges take a higher percentage of those who apply early. But the first wave of applicants tend to be more interested in a particular school, more likely to be legacies and recruited athletes. On the other hand, many kids who apply regular decision add a few schools almost randomly as insurance. Admissions offices sense that, and weed them out quickly, so the competition isn't quite as daunting in the general pool as the numbers sometimes imply.

Layla had studied hard to get into the best premed programs. She knew there were no guarantees, so she felt she should apply to a lot of schools to improve her chances.

She started with six, then eight, then a dozen, and ultimately picked twenty-eight, which Mr. Smith estimated was the longest list anyone had ever compiled at Oyster Bay.

S mitty kept track of Layla's college search through one of his "angels," who was Layla's counselor. Smitty was impressed with the girl's intellect. In tenth grade, she'd interviewed dozens of people to study how personality traits lead folks to pick their professions. She followed that with a detailed report about Oyster Bay's infamous resident, Typhoid Mary, whose contagiousness was discovered after she worked at a summer home early in the twentieth century. (Layla also made a fairly convincing case that Oyster Bay High was haunted.) Still, Smitty knew Layla well enough to be concerned about how she drove herself.

For a while, he assumed Layla was one of those kids who were too obsessed with grades. Then something happened that gave him a new insight. Over the summer, a computer error miscalculated Oyster Bay's grade point averages, so that Jenna appeared to be the valedictorian and Layla the salutatorian. Layla knew about the mistake, but said nothing. It took a complaint from a boy about his own GPA computation to prompt the school to correct the glitch. Layla moved up to her rightful spot as valedictorian. Later, Layla said she hadn't spoken up because she didn't want to make a fuss.

Smitty picked up another insight into Layla. She had told Kathi of traveling to Cambodia with her mother, and meeting a young man and woman who said they were trying to go to a college in the capital but couldn't afford the four-hundred-dollar tuition. Layla called the school, which confirmed their story. Using her own savings plus money from her mom, she wired the tuition payment.

Smitty was moved to see that Layla never mentioned this on her college applications. There were a few students like that. They wanted to view their volunteering as true service, not a selling point. But Smitty was not above marketing his kids. He made sure Layla's counselor included the Cambodia story in a recommendation letter.

Despite Layla's résumé, Smitty was skeptical about her chances at the toughest schools. Fifteen years ago, he knew, she would have been a slam dunk at almost any college, but 2008 was different. The race to get into the prestige places was so intense, with so many hyperperforming students, that a valedictorian label and excellent scores were no longer guarantees. Smitty saw one explanation in the College Board packets he received: The number of high school students taking Advanced Placement exams had soared 375 percent in fifteen years.

Every time Smitty checked in on Layla during the fall, it seemed she was tacking another college onto her list. That included second applications to schools that had seven-year med tracks and other separate programs with their own admissions process.

Layla pointed out that she'd gotten rid of a few possibilities. She'd briefly considered Harvard, but decided she didn't want to go there, and she had dropped Rochester, too. She kept a spreadsheet with the remaining names:

1. Siena College
2. Siena College—Albany Medical College program
3. George Washington University
4. George Washington University BA/MD
5. Adelphi University
6. Drew University
7. University of Miami
8. SUNY Geneseo
9. Emory University
10. Emory University's Oxford College: Honors program
11. New York University
12. Boston University
13. Stony Brook
14. Stony Brook: Honors College
15. Stony Brook: Women in Science and Engineering program
16. Stony Brook: BA/MD
17. Drexel University
18. Fordham University
19. Vanderbilt University

20. Columbia University

21. Brown University

22. Barnard College

23. University of Massachusetts at Amherst

24. American University

25. Northeastern University: Honors program

26. Muhlenberg College

27. McGill University

28. McGill University: Science program

Smitty considered the list too long and unfocused. Layla had chosen the two most different Ivies, Columbia with its mandatory core curriculum and Brown with its complete lack of requirements. She'd mixed in a little private college in Pennsylvania, Muhlenberg, with a giant state school in Massachusetts, UMass.

Smitty didn't like the shotgun approach because he preferred a common theme. Jeff, of all people, had realized that. He'd recently decided to apply only to schools with sports management or phys ed majors and strong basketball programs. He'd chosen eight, from Central Connecticut State to Towson in Maryland. His new priorities let him see that Fordham didn't fit, so he dropped it. Smitty wished more kids zeroed in like that, especially Layla.

"She's just hoping that one of the pellets hits a target," he remarked.

Still, she was hardly the only one with a long list. Plenty of students had well over a dozen. Like her, they did it because of the frenzied competition, but there were other reasons. Even the smallest colleges had stepped up marketing, and most offered virtual online tours that caught the interest of kids from afar. The Common Application, used by 350 colleges, made it simple to add schools. And families in need of aid packages felt they should try as many places as feasible.

The trend toward extensive application lists, Smitty thought, upped everyone's stress by making colleges appear more selective. Not long before, top schools still took one out of every five applicants, but now, many of those same places were taking one out of ten. It made for a vicious cycle, as anxious kids, seeing these long odds, applied to even more colleges. That was too bad, Smitty thought, because by the end of high school, a student's interests should ideally be converging on a narrower and more thoughtful list.

To establish balance, some counselors gave kids an "eight is enough" guideline. A few high schools even said they wouldn't process more than a dozen apps except in special circumstances.

Smitty agreed in principle, and yet he didn't push Layla to trim the list. It was her call. A few years earlier, at another district, he'd worked with a boy who insisted on twenty-one colleges, including all eight Ivies and Stanford, which is part of the elite "Ivy Deans' Group." Smitty suggested cutting the list, but the boy refused. All the Ivies turned him down, as did several other prestigious schools. Yet he was accepted to Stanford.

It taught Smitty that on rare occasions, the scattershot approach can work.

"If someone wanted to apply to fifty, I wouldn't agree," he remarked, "but I wouldn't stop it." Even so, Smitty worried that Layla's twenty-eight apps would force her to focus more on quantity than the quality of each package.

As December vacation approached, Layla finished her many essays. Kathi felt they needed work, but this being crunch time, she had her hands full with scores of compositions. She couldn't give the attention she'd been able to in October and November. She gently tried to tell Layla that her main essays needed thorough revisions, but Layla, too, was short of time.

Kathi didn't press it. She understood there comes a point when a student has decided to stop revising. The kids were the ones applying to college, after all. But Kathi did ask Smitty to take a look at Layla's work. At the least, she felt the prose was too flowery and needed toning down.

Smitty glanced at the essays. "My passion to become a psychiatrist was crystallized upon an experience I had," said one. Another was equally wordy: "My streams of academic interests act like beams converging on a smooth watery surface reflecting an image of the person I want to become." A third sounded more like a fortune cookie: "Every thousand miles I travel brings me one inch closer in my personal growth."

Smitty understood Kathi's concerns. He knew Layla could write better prose. But he decided it wouldn't help to say anything. Between her school activities and twenty-eight applications, Layla had enough pressure right now. Smitty, with deadlines at hand, did, too.

It had been another late night in the guidance cave. Smitty locked the door and headed out through the near-empty school.

As he walked down the hall to the exit, he could hear Layla, still typing away.

TWENTY-TWO

Apped-Out

Jeff Sanders, the youngest volunteer at Oyster Bay Fire Company No. 1, was fighting his first big blaze. It was at a restaurant. Smoke was billowing out when Jeff arrived on a hook and ladder truck shortly after midnight. He was assigned to get into the bucket with two other firemen. Soon, he was looking down at the roof, trying to decide where the fire might spread next. Jeff aimed a high-pressure spray gun, then squeezed the trigger.

"That's it!" one of the men yelled. The wind blew a mist back at them, forming ice on the metal bucket. Two-way radios echoed in the trucks below.

Jeff felt proud. When his dad was younger, he'd been a volunteer firefighter, and now Jeff was following tradition. Jeff liked to say he'd rather be busy than bored, and the last six hours were a good example. He'd arrived home from basketball practice in the evening, hung out with his young cousins, did his homework, and then went to a meeting at the firehouse. When a call came in for an emergency, Jeff all but begged the chief to let him suit up.

A few hours later, Jeff's first stop at school was the guidance office.

"Mr. Smith, guess what—"

Smitty listened and smiled, for more than one reason. Just as Jeff had made a breakthrough in his fire duties, he recently done so in class as well. Smitty was hearing back from teachers, the ones who had earlier noted Jeff's lagging performance. Lately, they said his grades were moving up.

The deadline for most regular applications was January 1. As Christmas vacation approached, Smitty kept reminding the students of that date. He told them the school would close on the afternoon of December 21, a Friday, and no guidance counselors would be around afterward to send out packets. By the time everyone returned to school on January 2, it would be too late.

One year, the guidance office had been swamped with applications the day before vacation, forcing the counselors and Blossom to work into the night. Looking back, Smitty wondered if that made for a few errors. He didn't want to repeat that during his last year on the job.

As suburban public schools had become more diverse, Smitty had to deal with unusual requests. Zara needed to finish all her applications quickly because she was flying to Saudi Arabia to take part in the hajj, the Muslim pilgrimage to Mecca, and would be out of touch for nearly a month. Adati had her own request: She wanted her packages to Penn State, Drexel, and other schools sent out on Wednesdays. She explained that like quite a few Sikhs from Punjab, her mother was superstitious and believed that Wednesdays were lucky.

One thing didn't change: Smitty found the mid-December frenzy the most hectic time of year. Whenever he stepped into Essay Writing for College, kids vied for his attention, wanting to check facts they needed for their forms.

"How many kids are in our senior class?" a girl asked.

"One hundred and nine," said Smitty.

"Do you know anything about the University of Tampa?" a boy called out.

"Yes is the short answer—"

Jeff interrupted. "Is it okay if I write about sports for the C. W. Post application?"

"It depends," Smitty replied. "You can if you block those metaphors." He reminded Jeff that most sports essays turn out to be clichés.

He turned back to the boy who had asked about UTampa. "That campus is a jewel," Smitty enthused.

Other kids kept pulling at him. It was all about deadline jitters. At times, Smitty felt like he'd walked into a kindergarten class.

"But Mr. Smith?" It was Jeff again. He wanted to know—should he write about sports or not?

"Usually kids write about a generic experience in sports," Smitty said. But he knew that Jeff had quarterbacked the football team to the playoffs—the first time Oyster Bay had gotten that far in years. That, Smitty said, could be the start of a piece.

Smitty liked seeing this new, more diligent Jeff Sanders. Something had finally clicked inside him. Teachers even said he was calmer in class. At one point, he told Smitty that a certain younger kid on the basketball team needed to get serious about school. Smitty tried not to say anything. That sounded like the advice he'd been giving Jeff since the start of this year.

Jeff was following Smitty's counsel on his essays as well. The latest one began with sports, but revealed Jeff's dedication. "Basketball is my love, my passion, possibly my obsession," Jeff started. He wrote about watching coaches during games, and trying to outguess them. "I wasn't blessed with Division I basketball talent, but I was certainly blessed with a Division I basketball brain."

Jeff was a good example of why Smitty didn't write recommendations in September, as some counselors do. Waiting paid off. Having just recently seen Jeff come into his own, he was now able to capture him at his best.

Smitty's first paragraph explained why fourteen people lived in the Sanders house. Then he told of urging Jeff to take tougher math and science courses, and how Jeff raised his first set of senior grades to high Bs.

"You need to know that he had a 50 in precalculus, a 70 in physics, a 72 in Spanish 5H, and an 80 in English 12 on his progress report. Look at what he accomplished in five weeks!"

Just that morning, Smitty added, Jeff had come to school after answering a call as a fire department volunteer. Smitty concluded: "He represents all that is right with today's youth."

Riana Tyson, too, was starting to deliver, and Smitty worked with Matt Brown to keep her going. Matt told her to stop showing up at SADD meetings for a few weeks because she needed time for schoolwork and college apps. She couldn't help anyone else, Matt said, till she started helping herself.

Meanwhile, Smitty gave Riana a timeline showing when to have her essays ready. Over Thanksgiving break, Matt had called her to make sure she was following it.

One by one, she finished her applications before deadline: Georgia Tech, University of Miami, Northeastern, Pitt, Temple, Fordham, and—in part because Mr. Smith kept talking about it—the City College of New York.

She hadn't planned on applying to a historically black college, but she liked what she'd read about Spelman as well as the city where it was located, Atlanta. She sent a packet there, too. That made eight schools.

Riana hadn't yet visited any of them. Travel was difficult because she worked weekends and her mom put in long hours during the week. In late November, things suddenly got worse for the Tysons when her mother's company went bankrupt and all the employees lost their jobs.

Smitty knew this would have a big impact on Riana's choices. He called the family's home to promise he would do everything possible to get Riana financial aid. Meanwhile, he assured the Tysons she had some affordable colleges on her list.

Riana seemed to handle the situation with grace. She was even dispensing some advice herself. She encouraged Andreas Dukas, her friend from physics class, to look at Georgia Tech. Andreas had figured he'd go to a local college, or maybe Binghamton in upstate New York. But he read up on Georgia Tech and it struck him as the kind of place where it was all right to be a science geek. He applied.

When the kids in room 207 were at last done with their applications, Kathi urged most to move on to scholarship essays. It wasn't easy. They'd been at this for three and a half months. They were apped-out. During one class, a couple of kids, needing a distraction, tried to find the most oddball scholarship. They came across one for left-handed students, and another from something called the National Association to Advance Fat Acceptance, offering one thousand dollars for the best essay on accepting fat people. A third, sponsored by the manufacturers of duct tape, asked for photos of kids who went to prom in outfits made of their product. The winners would get three thousand dollars.

Smitty had seen kids get a little "out there" on their essays, too. One night, Kathi showed him a piece by a student on a notable UVA question: "Write about a favorite word." Smitty was taken aback when he read the first word:

"Ass."

But the student developed the essay well, and Smitty knew it would attract more attention than the painfully predictable words many use, like *charity* and *philanthropy*.

Just to be sure, Kathi called a nephew with contacts at UVA admissions. She reported his findings to Smitty: "Last year, four kids wrote about the *F* word." Two got in, two did not.

Lee Kim was apped-out, too, and he'd finished only a few of his twenty-one packages. He hadn't heard from Oxford yet, and showed little enthusiasm about the colleges picked by his parents. Although he had barely begun, he was ready for the process to be over. He ran out of inspiration when yet another school asked him to explain why he wanted to go there. He turned to Dominique, sitting next him.

"Would you please tell me why I am interested in their academic program?"

Dominique suggested a one-sentence answer: "I want to make money." That's what Lee himself had often told her when he talked about college.

He smiled at hearing his own words quoted back at him.

"Can you tell me something that doesn't make me sound like a pompous ass?" he said.

"I'm sorry, Lee," she deadpanned. "I have to be honest." Then she started singing "For the Love of Money," by the O'Jays, stretching out the lyrics: *"Money, money, money, money . . ."*

But Lee wasn't kidding. He needed someone, anyone, to tell him why he was applying to this latest college. "Would you please—" he began.

"I'm looking, I'm looking!" Dominique pulled up Google, and did a search for "Ways to say I love money without sounding obnoxious."

Nathaniel Coleman made a resolution: He would not get weighed down by the application frenzy anymore. He was going to start having some fun. For too much of high school, he told himself, he'd stayed home studying while other kids partied. Before senior year, during the times he did decide to unwind, he often turned to video games. "It was more or less just a form of escapism," he admitted, "pretending to be someone you're not for a little bit just so you can get away from what you have to face."

Now he was going to get out more. It felt great to think about it. And yet even as he vowed to do so, he knew that with Columbia having rejected him, he had to get new applications finished. He had a list of six with good engineering departments: Tufts, Cornell, Rensselaer Polytechnic Institute, Worcester Polytechnic Institute, Northeastern, and Boston U.

Sitting in room 207 during fourth period, studying a list of essay questions he had yet to tackle, he didn't appear to be someone who was having fun.

"Looking at this," he said, "makes me want to throw up."

On the last school day in December, most of the seniors were in an upbeat mood. Kathi played Cranium with her AP class, and Chelsea Flynn arrived with a box of cupcakes she'd baked. A dozen chorus members went from classroom to classroom singing carols, finally stopping at the guidance cave. Lee was in the middle, and Smitty noticed him beaming as he sang "Joy to the World." Smitty had seen that same look when Lee played in the orchestra and the jazz ensemble, but not when he sat in Essay Writing for College.

Lee nodded at Smitty and kept singing. He didn't let on that he'd recently received his first college decision: a rejection from Oxford.

Nathaniel sank into a chair in Deanna's office. He ran a hand through his unkempt hair as he told Deanna his mother had said he couldn't go on the family ski trip.

"What did you do wrong, Nathaniel?" Deanna asked.

"I was rejected by Columbia."

Deanna was incredulous. "Your mom is punishing you for not getting into Columbia?"

Nathaniel wasn't certain, but that's how he'd understood it. He was now about to send applications to Cornell, Duke, and Boston University. On top of those, his mom had come up with a list of ten more colleges that had applications due in January.

Deanna tried to keep an even tone.

"Nathaniel," she said, "your mother cannot fault you for a decision by an admissions office. . . ."

She went next door to Smitty's office, closed his door, and told him what Nathaniel's mom was doing.

"She's what?" Smitty's cheeks turned color. "It's vindictive. He hasn't failed."

In the last few years, he'd seen parents grow increasingly zealous about the college chase. The previous fall, when everyone knew counselors were writing recommendations, a senior gave Smitty a card with a five-hundred-dollar gift certificate to Bloomingdale's.

He called the boy in and handed it back. "I'm going to trust that you'll return it to your father," Smitty said, adding that he doubted it was the student's idea.

They turned to Nathaniel's prospects. Deanna was optimistic about his chances at other top schools. "I think he'd be great at a BU or an NYU."

"He won't get into NYU," said Smitty. "At best he'll be wait-listed."

Deanna was about to ask how Smitty knew that, but he read her thoughts and pointed to his gray hair. They both agreed that Nathaniel had a great chance of getting into BU, but Smitty questioned whether the urban campus would be a good fit. He thought Nathaniel would do better at a small school where he wouldn't get lost.

Deanna asked what she should say to Nathaniel's mother.

Smitty didn't hesitate. His cheeks and ears turned crimson, as happened when he was frustrated.

"Tell her this: 'Punishing your son will have consequences for your long-term relationship with him.'"

At the end of the school day, Deanna returned to Smitty's office. She was not her usual cheerful self.

"Nathaniel's mom?" Smitty asked.

Yes, Nathaniel's mom.

Deanna had met with her, and asked her not to make Nathaniel apply to ten more schools over vacation. One of those additions, Deanna pointed out, was Georgetown University, which didn't even have an engineering program.

The mom was very pleasant, Deanna said. They'd reduced the ten schools to three. Still, the mom wasn't going to reinstate the ski trip. She told Deanna she'd canceled the trip so that Nathaniel would have time to work on the extra apps.

Smitty reminded Deanna that Nathaniel did have some good news. The University of Vermont had already accepted him. That might not be the family's first choice, but it was a great place for a smart kid who liked the outdoors. No matter what happened with Nathaniel's list of top engineering schools, the youngster had a fine backup.

But Deanna knew he was still feeling pressure. Of course, it wasn't just Nathaniel. Many kids were in limbo at this time of year, waiting another two or three months to find out where they'd get accepted. The holidays gave relatives plenty of opportunities to ask the question that couldn't yet be answered.

At home that night, Smitty and Kathi sat by the fireplace with gifts of cologne, notepads, and bath products from the kids. The two chuckled as they read the cards. They were like miniature application essays. In two or three sentences, each student's personality came through. Adati was bubbly. "Lovey," she wrote to Kathi, "I hope someday I can party with you . . . Partying with an English teacher?"

Kasper had given Smitty a pair of black leather gloves. He wrote that he would always remember the day he heard that Smitty would be his counselor. His mother and he were overjoyed, and Kasper had told his father of Smitty's reputation.

Smitty read the note to Kathi:

"Mr. Smith," Kasper wrote of NYU, "you have done your wonders to get me into my dream school, making me the happiest person ever. Most importantly, however, you helped me make my dad proud."

Earlier that day, Riana had stopped by Smitty's office. Like Jeff, she had shown impressive growth in the last months. She had energized SADD, and had helped her classmate Andreas come out of his shell to talk about the death of his brother. She even played guidance counselor in his case, encouraging him to apply to Georgia Tech, although he insisted that he wanted to stay in New York State. It occurred to Smitty she might make a good counselor herself someday.

Smitty saw she had a box in her hand. She told him it was a Christmas present.

"Can you open it now?" she asked.

It was a mug with the insignia of his adored New York Jets.

He read the card:

"You have shown me opportunities that I couldn't have imagined were there for me," it began.

Smitty read on. "I have found a mentor I will never forget. Love, Riana."

He had to pause for a second before thanking her. A moment later, she was on her way.

Smitty watched her walk off, hoping she knew just how much she had to offer.

TWENTY-THREE

It Takes a Village to Write an Essay

The final deadline was at hand. It was January 15, when the last big round of regular-decision applications were due. For those seniors who had yet to finish, it was the only priority. Chelsea Flynn was among them. She had sent packages to eight colleges, but still had three to go today: NYU, Middlebury, and Skidmore.

As Chelsea walked into the guidance office, she saw it had turned into a staging area for the home stretch. Nathaniel Coleman and a couple of other kids were working on their apps.

Chelsea was wearing a white button-down shirt and jeans tucked into her boots. She wore a bracelet with the word "Rhine," which means "flow" in German, her symbol of how she wanted to approach life, but not this week.

Like many of her classmates, she was tired of filling out forms and revising essays. It was her nature to redo things until they were perfect, which was one reason she wasn't finished. She took a MacBook out of her leather purse, opened the screen, and got to work.

Although Chelsea said she resented the admissions race, Smitty believed it had forced her to sort out larger issues about herself. Did she want to be near her family or strike out on her own? Did she see herself in an urban school like NYU or on a more provincial campus? She was starting to answer those questions. She had at first been interested in remote Spring Hill in Alabama because one of her uncles recommended it highly, but she visited and didn't like the school's religious emphasis.

Chelsea sat down and went to work, first finishing a few details on her Middlebury application. Soon, it was ready to go. Smitty prepared to send it. Until he pressed the button, he half expected her to say she'd decided on one more change, but she had already moved on to Skidmore.

She printed out a short essay explaining why it would be a good match for her. She wrote that she liked the idea of sampling Skidmore's variety. That approach didn't do much for Smitty. It wasn't *Chelsea* enough. But today was January 15, and though the piece wasn't perfect, it was done. Smitty proofread the application while Chelsea ate a granola bar. They agreed it was in order. She clicked SUBMIT.

NYU was next. One of the school's short essays asked for a description of a campus group the applicant would like to start. Smitty had seen plenty of pat answers to that as students wrote earnestly about clubs that would feed the homeless or help the needy.

Smitty liked Chelsea's answer: She'd start a "disposable art" club, encouraging students to create colorful drawings and write messages in chalk on the pavement. "The pieces and sayings exist until the rain washes them away," she explained.

Soon, NYU's app was sent, too. But Chelsea wasn't done. She reminded Smitty that she had one application left, with a February 1 deadline. It was to Hobart and William Smith upstate. Smitty sighed and said he'd see her in two weeks.

Sitting inside the guidance suite, Deanna reread one of Nathaniel's sentences out loud: "My thoughts stay accurate."

She glanced up at him. "I thought we changed that," she said.

Nathaniel said he thought they had, too.

Deanna leaned back and rubbed her eyes. "I have never revised one line so many times in my life," she said.

Nathaniel insisted he had to make one more adjustment. He wanted to find a place to add a semicolon. "I'm semicolon-happy," he said. "I just learned what they were." He inserted two semicolons, and looked pleased.

To Deanna, Nathaniel seemed like a little kid in a seventeen-year-old's body. He was on a life-changing deadline and yet still had to play.

After Columbia's rejection, Nathaniel had to find his way again. His best friend, Evan, also wanted to be an engineer, and both were applying to Worcester Polytechnic Institute, Rensselaer Polytechnic, and Carnegie Mellon. Nathaniel also applied to Cornell, which had accepted five of seven Oyster Bay applicants the previous year. On a visit, he'd liked Ithaca, with its gorges and views of Cayuga Lake. "The scenery is amazing," he said.

Nathaniel had one main essay that he adjusted for different colleges. It had gone through countless drafts, with input from a guidance counselor, a teacher, Nathaniel's parents, and Nathaniel himself.

He had managed to preserve his opening: "Ever since I could walk, I had an inner energy and liveliness. I was never able to sit still. I was always moving, thinking, and dreaming."

Nathaniel went on to recount the time he'd assembled an intricate Lego Star Wars model—a nice early glimpse, Deanna thought, into his engineering personality. He added some humor, too. One day, he found the model shattered on the floor. He tried to figure out who had wrecked it and realized it was his cat. An appealing touch, Deanna thought. She suspected admissions officers don't see many funny engineers.

He finished adjusting the essay for Case Western, then for NYU. He was done. He put on his jacket and lifted his backpack. He'd just completed his last application ever.

Well, at least until graduate school, he said.

"Then I've got to do it all again, dammit."

Lee Kim came in to see Smitty at 1:55 p.m., twenty-one minutes before the end of classes on deadline day. He'd called in sick at the start of school so he could stay home working on apps, and now he was in for some editing help.

NYU's submission, he felt, had been easy. He told Smitty he'd dashed off the five miniessays in a few minutes. He was ready to click the SUBMIT button.

Smitty wanted him to slow down. Could they please first proofread it?

Smitty liked to see how different kids answered the same essay question. He checked Lee's piece describing his idea for a new student club. Lee proposed a vending service selling low-cost food at NYU's library. Smitty liked that—Chelsea showed her artsy side, and Lee showed his mix of business and idealism.

Lee pushed the button, and off it went to NYU. He had one more to go, to little-known Deep Springs out west. Oddly, Lee was more excited about Deep Springs than about any of the others, including the five Ivies on his list.

Several hundred boys had applied to Deep Springs for a mere thirteen spots, and the school had narrowed the pool to forty finalists, Lee among them. As a result, he had to write three more essays, then go on a campus visit to do interviews and the kind of farm chores that are part of the curriculum there. He would fly into Nevada and take buses to the campus in the California desert north of Death Valley.

Lee asked Smitty to call to see if the school had received his recommendations and final transcript. Smitty wasn't paying attention to the time, and at first thought it was too early out west. Lee assured him there was no such thing as "too early" at a college that was part of a ranch. "They get up at four to milk cows," he explained.

"I don't know if they have phones next to the cows," Smitty replied. But he made the call because Lee was antsy. Smitty got through. Yes, Deep Springs had all the guidance office's paperwork.

In one of the essays, Deep Springs asked the finalists to discuss a problem or theory. Lee wrote about how in tenth grade, he began doubting religion even as he served as an altar boy during Christmas Mass. He described his thoughts that day as he watched a younger kid rotely reading aloud phrases from the Bible: "I saw myself in the shoes of that little boy with his finger stuck up his nose."

Lee said he had done the exact same thing for fourteen years. "Of course," he added whimsically, "periodically I took my finger out of my nose."

Smitty leaned back in his chair, the essay in his hand. He liked the mix of introspection and wit. Lee had approached an intense topic in a way that kept it from being too heavy. And Smitty appreciated some edgy phrases that many parents might have censored, like this one:

"I proclaimed 'God bless you' whenever I heard a sneeze and 'God damn it' whenever I stubbed my toe."

Admissions officers, Smitty knew, see few lines like that. It could help Lee stand out.

A bell sounded to end ninth period. The day was done. Hunched over printouts in the guidance cave, Smitty and Lee could hear kids shouting as they headed home.

Smitty looked up from the essay. It was one of the more sophisticated compositions anyone in the class had written. "Fantastic," he said. No doubt it would give Lee plenty to talk about in the admissions interview at Deep Springs.

Lee moved on to finish the other Deep Springs pieces. The college was one of few that still asked for applications on paper, so they had to get it in the mail. It was now four P.M., past Oyster Bay High's last postal pickup. Smitty went online and told Lee he had found a nearby post office that stayed open until 11:30.

Lee said he'd like Smitty's advice on something. "My mom wants to come with me, and I don't want her to." He was talking about the Deep Springs visit.

"Why not?"

"She'd be a distraction." Lee didn't want his mother shadowing him. The school's mission was to teach self-sufficiency, and he felt it would be a bad start to show up with his mom. Smitty wasn't sure. Perhaps Lee would be more comfortable not having to make the long trip alone. But if she made him uptight, that was no good. Smitty knew that Lee needed to be relaxed when interacting with college reps, because he'd shown prickliness in the past.

Not long before, Lee had arranged to meet a Princeton graduate for an alum interview at a Starbucks. Traditionally, the alum is supposed to do the judging, but in this case, Lee sounded judgmental. "I'm not going to lie," he told Smitty afterward. "He seemed kind of boring and awkward."

Smitty shook his head in wonder. Surely a bright teenager who'd traveled to Bosnia could have found something in common with a Princeton alum. Smitty didn't think alum interviews could improve an applicant's chances, but he felt a negative comment from an interviewer could hurt.

Smitty made a mental note: Forget Princeton.

Lee had ended his applications season just the way he'd started the previous spring: by perplexing his guidance counselor. In the end, Lee had applied to twenty-one places. Besides Oxford and Princeton, he'd gone for Amherst, Bentley, Binghamton, University of Chicago, Columbia, Cornell, Dartmouth, Deep Springs, Duke, Harvard, UMass, McGill, NYU–Stern School of Business, Northwestern, U Penn, Stanford, Swarthmore, Vanderbilt, and Yale.

Lee gathered the essays for his Deep Springs application and went home to polish them. That left Smitty to talk with Kathi, who'd stopped by the guidance office. Smitty blamed himself for not giving Lee more direction in the past few months. Lee had appeared so in control that it was easy to forget he was still a kid. In some ways, he was also a question mark. Here was a brilliant boy who had a shot at Ivies but was more interested in a tiny college in the desert. That was fine, even laudable, as long as it was for the right reasons. Was it? Smitty wasn't sure yet.

By now, the school was mostly empty, the deadline rush done. In all, the 109 seniors had sent out 661 applications to 216 colleges. The schools ranged from Nassau Community College around the corner to Stanford in Palo Alto. While the majority were clustered in the Boston-Washington corridor, there had been bids for schools from Miami to San Diego, from Canada to England.

Except for a very few places with a February deadline, the Oyster Bay High class of 2008 had finished applying to college.

TWENTY-FOUR

The $250,000 Question

On a Monday evening in late January, thirty mothers and fathers sat in the computer room armed with documents they'd need for the next phase of the college chase: tax returns and financial statements.

Smitty greeted them with good news: All their kids' applications were done.

Then the bad: The hard part would now begin. They had to figure out how to pay for college.

In Smitty's nine years at the school, this was a record turnout for a financial aid workshop. The parents were a cross-section of Oyster Bay: business owners, a house painter, even a clammer. They were white, Hispanic, Asian, and black; their children were considering two- and four-year schools, public and private.

To Smitty, the big crowd was an economic indicator: More families than ever were struggling to find the money for college.

The cost of higher education, he knew, had never been greater.

Sending one child to the most expensive schools for four years could run nearly $250,000 including extras and inflation. It was daunting not just for the middle and working-class but also for those once considered prosperous. Harvard had recently decided that even families making $180,000 a year should be eligible for tuition assistance.

And what about those who didn't get enough financial assistance? The parents of two Oyster Bay kids accepted early to out-of-state colleges had already told Smitty the aid packages they'd been offered wouldn't cover their costs, so they were going to choose a New York State school instead. He was sure others would be forced to make a similar choice.

"Some of you have been through this before, so you're experts," Smitty said, glancing at Chelsea's mom and dad. They had attended the workshop a year earlier for their oldest daughter, and after Chelsea they still had two younger kids. That would make for sixteen years of tuition payments— Smitty couldn't quite comprehend that.

Kasper's mother was there, needing to figure out finances alone now that she was a widow. Curtis's mom came, too. She had struggled since her husband left the family. Smitty hoped Curtis would be admitted to the University of Miami, his top choice, but he'd need a significant package to afford it.

Smitty understood that borrowing wasn't the simple answer some folks assumed. He knew of parents who felt they could handle $30,000 annual loans, but four years later were struggling with $120,000 of debt, with thousands in annual interest. And the burden often started sooner than that. Smitty reminded his audience that the first payments on some loans are due when the money is borrowed, not at graduation. "So your child has one heck of a nut to pay off before getting started in life," he said.

Smitty turned over the presentation to a friend who had worked in the financial aid office of several colleges. On a screen, he projected a key document—the FAFSA, or Free Application for Federal Student Aid.

It lets families enter their salaries, savings, and investments to calculate how much they would be expected to pay.

Some parents began to do the computations in their heads. One father groaned.

Families with fewer resources, said Smitty, must even think about what jobs their kids might choose after graduation. A student who planned on a service career such as social work, he pointed out, should not take on big loans.

The conferences Smitty attended often discussed the larger issue of a college's effect on the earning power of grads. Some argued that the very top schools put kids way out front. One study found that those who attend the "most competitive" schools earn 21 to 23 percent more than those who go to "very competitive" colleges. A Harvard economist examined why, and found that the key was the ability to network with accomplished students, alumni, professors, and campus visitors.

But Smitty gave more credence to a Wharton School study that showed a changing trend. In 1980, 32 percent of American CEOs had degrees from public colleges and universities. By 2000, that was up to 48 percent. In another investigation, a Princeton researcher found virtually no earnings difference fifteen years out of Ivy and public universities.

Whichever study was right, Smitty felt, there was one main concern here: Be wary of starting life after college with too much debt.

More immediately, Smitty's job now was to see what aid he could get for individual kids—not just through admissions packages but through private scholarships. Students in Essay Writing for College had to look at www.finaid.org, a site that described scores of them.

A good example to Smitty was the five-thousand-dollar scholarship given annually to an Oyster Bay athlete to honor a coach who had died.

Money like this was out there, he said, if you looked hard. In this case, he'd written a confidential note to the family that set up the scholarship saying he'd found the right student—a young man who captained the football and basketball teams and volunteered for the fire department.

But Jeff was just one of dozens who needed help, and Smitty glanced around the audience, thinking about other matches.

The discussion continued into the evening. The parents kept asking questions: What if a stepparent has savings? Are a teenager's earnings considered? What if your house is now worth less than its assessment?

Smitty always found this a sobering evening. He would watch as various parents realized that getting accepted didn't mean their child would be able to go.

For several days in a row, Curtis came to Kathi's class and headed straight for a computer. In the first four months of school, the room was used to apply to colleges, now it was used to apply for money. Curtis's mom had found a scholarship offered by the Horatio Alger Association that she thought he should try for. It provided twenty thousand dollars over four years, but the odds were tough: Thirty thousand high school seniors competed annually for only one hundred of them.

Curtis didn't mind long odds. When he'd had meningitis as a child, doctors questioned whether he would walk again. Now he captained the tennis team.

The application required three essays, and Curtis did them quickly. Kathi felt he'd gained confidence from writing his college compositions, and was now comfortable talking honestly. One of the Horatio Alger essays asked about adversities.

"My problems are not who I am," Curtis began. "Sure, my father left my mother, brother, and me with just about zero money in the bank, and without any notice."

Kathi liked the conversational voice. She felt it connected better than the more formal tone kids usually use with school papers.

"I was paralyzed from the waist down when I was three years old," he wrote. "Yes, I did have five agonizing surgeries over the past two years on my feet to correct the deformity from the paralysis."

As for his recuperation, instead of dwelling on what he was missing, Curtis wrote that the downtime taught him to enjoy a simpler life. He concluded: "My problems are not who I am. My problems are what helped make me a stronger person."

Despite his optimism, Curtis had low periods. One day, looking glum he stopped by to see Smitty. He said he and his mom had to move to a smaller apartment to save money.

Smitty started to ask if he could help, but Curtis shrugged in a way that said he was just venting, not asking for anything. He knew he and his mom would get through this, too.

For years, parents had told Smitty that if a college didn't work out, their child could always transfer. Smitty couldn't argue; he'd done it twice himself. Surveys showed that a surprising 40 percent of those graduating college had begun at a different institution.

But as college costs rose, transferring was tougher. Private colleges gave the best aid packages to students who committed to four years. Transfers got whatever was left, if anything. These days, most Oyster Bay alumni who switched went from a private college to a public one.

Because of the state of the economy, some families talked about deferring college for a year. That was fine with Smitty. He had long felt that many kids could benefit from a pause. For those uncertain about what they wanted to do in life, Smitty sometimes recommended a community college. A stop at a two-year school could help them improve study habits and think about careers. He also knew that many private-school kids, mostly athletes, do a postgraduate year as second-time seniors at a boarding school to improve their game and grades.

Just as often, Smitty suggested a gap year—a break from school to hold a job, do service, or put on a backpack and explore. Smitty found this could be a hard sell to parents, but he still pushed for it, and lately, with the stock market and savings accounts down, it had a pragmatic twist. To afford college, some kids needed to work a year to save up.

Essay Writing for College was a half-year elective, and it ended in January. In the last few days, Kathi and Smitty assigned the class an exercise they considered critical.

Good high schools prepare kids for college academic work, but almost none, Smitty had come to see, taught kids about managing their day-to-day lives after leaving home. That often led to problems. One study found that the average college senior carries a credit card debt of more than three thousand dollars. Smitty wanted them to know what they faced. It was time to get practical.

Kathi took the lead and asked the students to figure out how much it would cost to buy clothes and decorate a dorm room. She told them to go online and fill an electronic cart to see.

During first period, Chelsea, Jeff, Lee, and Dominique went onto the Bed Bath & Beyond Web site and pored over images of sheets and towels.

The kids were soon surprised.

"Three hundred and forty dollars," one murmured.

They added more items.

"Five hundred and sixty-three."

"Two thousand seventy-nine!"

Smitty considered this final part of class to be serious business. He even had the manager of a local bank branch come to talk about checking accounts and loans.

Nor did he stop at matters of money. Smitty had long believed that life skills should be taught along with math and chemistry. That included daily tasks that adults mistakenly assume eighteen-year-olds understand. Smitty had heard of more than a few college freshmen, mostly boys, who arrived on campus with no idea how to use a washing machine.

That brought Kathi and Smitty to the final homework assignment: The kids had to clean their rooms, cook dinner for their families, and then document the experiences with photos and essays.

Smitty and Kathi were always amused when the assignment came back, and this year they weren't disappointed.

Chelsea arranged her report in storybook form. "The day began like any other," she wrote over a picture of the mounds of clothes in her room. "But today I would have to clean."

Then came the "after" shot—a photo of herself grinning at her own progress. She wrote that it was the first time she had seen her floor in two weeks.

She went on to document her kitchen skills, talking up her dinner of couscous and chicken breasts sautéed with garlic, dill, and lemon pepper. The report proudly concluded: "Mission accomplished!"

Others had a similar approach. With her flair for drama, Dominique found a novel way to show she had become the model homemaker. She handed in a report trimmed with ribbons, and featuring pictures of herself in a Martha Stewart wig.

Kathi and Smitty knew the kids would take it lightheartedly. That was fine. But it was their job to prepare these students for college. Making

sure they could prepare dinner and understand a bank statement was part
of it. Smitty's last Essay Writing class was over.

A few weeks after Curtis mentioned he had to move to a smaller
apartment, he walked into Smitty's office with good news.

"Remember the Horatio Alger scholarship?"

Smitty did remember.

"I won it!"

The scholarship was worth $5,000 a year, and Curtis was one of a hun-
dred recipients in the country. They would even be flying him to Washington to receive the award at a dinner. "My mother was so excited, she
couldn't stop crying," he said.

Smitty did some quick math in his head and whistled. He knew that
Curtis's first choice, the University of Miami, matched scholarships. The
$20,000 would double to $40,000 if he was accepted—$10,000 a year.
That would make it affordable for him.

There are many advantaged kids, Smitty thought, who achieve a dream
by getting into an Ivy, but if a boy from a single-parent household could
get into the University of Miami, it could truly change his life.

With his gray-haired instincts, Smitty was fairly sure Curtis would be
accepted there. He had the scores, and he had outstanding recs. Smitty
did have one concern. It wasn't always easy for a northeastern youngster to
adjust to Florida, or a boy of modest means like Curtis to fit into a school
known as a party place for the privileged. But Curtis needed that scholarship. Smitty was counting on it being the right fit.

TWENTY-FIVE

"It's About Growing Up"

Upon returning from their college visits, many of the kids at Oyster Bay exchanged stories about dorms with walk-in closets, sushi in the dining halls, or state-of-the-art science buildings. Lee Kim had nothing like that after his trip to Deep Springs.

How could he describe a school where kids got up at five A.M. to milk cows? Where they sheared sheep before classes, and scrubbed pots after meals? He did try. At one point, while telling a girl about the henhouse and the surrounding California desert, she looked at him like he was nuts.

This was a *college*?

Another asked, "Why would you want to be a cowboy?" It's not how they pictured their cerebral classmate who studied at a Korean school on Saturdays. But Lee Kim had decided Deep Springs was exactly where he belonged.

In the Korean community, many families wanted their children to shoot for a top school, and dutifully, Lee had applied to more than half of the Ivy League. But he saw Deep Springs as a way to make his own path. A part of him even thought that if Harvard said yes, he might say no.

Most kids became more sure of themselves as they worked through the college search. For a while, Lee seemed to become only more conflicted. He ultimately applied to twenty-one schools—a sign that he had little idea where he wanted to go, Smitty thought.

Early on, Lee's dad had offered to buy him the car of his choice if he took the SATs again and upped his scores to perfect 800s—what some admissions people called "dialing toll-free." But Lee kept putting off the tests. What was the point? So he could say he got into an elite university? He preferred looking for a place that excited him. He found it in Deep Springs.

For starters, he loved how different it was. The college offered its student body of twenty-six boys two years of manual labor and intellectual debate. All got full scholarships, the equivalent, the school said, of fifty thousand dollars a year. Deep Springs noted that afterward, they often were prime candidates to transfer as juniors to a college.

When Lee got back from California on a Monday in mid-February, Smitty checked in briefly with him in room 207.

"Give me, on a scale of one to ten, how you felt about Deep Springs."

"Fourteen," Lee responded.

To Smitty, it made a certain kind of sense. In Lee's community, and family, a school like Harvard remained the ideal, but Lee's own father had picked out Deep Springs as another option, probably with some wisdom. It allowed Lee to go his own way, to buck the system, and yet it could lead to a leading university. In Lee's case, if there was such a thing as respectable rebellion, Deep Springs would be it.

Smitty suspected that a bit of the allure of Deep Springs lay in its daunting acceptance rate. Lee might act above the college chase, but a part of him liked the idea of making one of the toughest cuts of all.

Smitty would have to wait to hear more. That Monday afternoon, Lee left school early with a fever. He went to a doctor, who said the stress of Lee's college search had resulted in a bout of bronchitis.

Of all the seniors Smitty dealt with, Lee was the toughest to understand. The boy was brilliant, but sometimes he sabotaged himself.

At one point, he had an offer to do an interview with a Vanderbilt alum who lived nearby, but at first Lee refused. He had some inexplicable unease about going to a stranger's house. And there was the time he went for that Princeton interview, but made little effort because the alum hadn't impressed him enough.

Sometimes, Lee did recognize his flaws. Oyster Bay's student newspaper once interviewed him for a story about a youth leadership program he attended. "It opened my eyes to my own arrogance," Lee told the paper.

Smitty was surprised at how critically Lee could look at himself. Lee tended to hold himself apart at school, but Smitty felt that on some level, he longed for connection.

As it became more likely that Lee could actually end up at Deep Springs, Smitty studied its Web site closely. He began to understand the school's appeal to Lee. Aside from the farm chores, it had a rigorous intellectual atmosphere.

"At every hour of the day," the site said, "there are at least a few people awake and discussing Heidegger, playing chess, or strumming guitars."

Lee had a need to be different but still cerebral, and Deep Springs offered that. For the right kind of kid, thought Smitty—one who was ready for neither a mainstream college nor a traditional gap year—this was a compelling third choice.

In the marathon of college admissions, February is a slow spell for high school seniors. By then, applications and financial aid forms are in. A few kids go on campus visits, alum interviews, and get rolling admission answers, but compared to the first semester, and the January deadline rush, it's a respite. Mostly, the seniors waited for March and April.

It was a time when even Smitty could focus on some of the routine gossip of high school. He and Kathi noticed that Riana had lately looked great and seemed more relaxed. Matt Brown said that she was dating Andreas. Their connection had started junior year in physics class, and it had continued at the Tuesday night meetings of SADD and Undecided.

Smitty saw Riana and Andreas as quiet kids who had been holding themselves back a bit in school, which he thought was unfortunate because both had so much to give. "They're going to bring out the best in each other," Matt predicted.

Andreas had given Riana a present: a book of images from the Hubble Space Telescope. She thought it was the perfect gift.

Lee returned to the guidance cave after a week to talk with Smitty about his visit to Deep Springs.

"I'm starting at base zero," Smitty said. He knew nothing and wanted to hear everything.

Lee described the journey west—two flights to get to Reno, then a pair of bus rides through Nevada to a stop at the California border, where he met two other boys who were finalists. A Deep Springs van picked the three up and drove the last hour to the school.

The buildings were simple and looked more like a ranch than a college.

There was even a blacksmith shop. It was as remote a campus as Lee could have imagined.

"Tuesday morning, I was home watching the news on TV," Lee said, "and Tuesday night I had no idea what was going on in the outside world."

Smitty asked him to describe the place.

Lee said it was stark and beautiful, surrounded by alfalfa fields and the distant Inyo Mountains. He particularly loved the night sky, sharp and clear without New York's light pollution.

"I spent five minutes looking for constellations," he told Smitty, "and in those five minutes I saw five shooting stars."

"And the town itself?"

"There is no town."

That evening, Lee said, several kids gave ten-minute orations as part of a public-speaking class. Close to midnight, Lee went out with one of the students to watch him work as a butcher. Later still, at the bunkhouse, he stayed up talking to a boy who played the harp as Lee sang Mozart arias until two in the morning. That was typical of Deep Springs.

"Were these the kind of kids you could connect with?" asked Smitty.

Lee excitedly said that they were. "They're always thinking about things," he told Smitty, "providing counterarguments."

That, he added, was part of the school's philosophy—to encourage vibrant debate about societal issues.

Lee also said the school wasn't a perfect model of clean living; he found a plastic bin filled with empty liquor bottles. His dad had liked the no-drugs-or-alcohol policy, but, as with other schools, kids sometimes sneaked things into their rooms after outside visits. Still, it was the opposite of the typical college party scene.

Lee described the boy assigned as his host, a student who had transferred from the University of Chicago. He had promised his host he'd help with chores at seven the next morning, but woke up an hour late. He had set his watch for the wrong time zone. Still, there were plenty of chores left to do. He fed a calf with a milk bottle, and worked in the dairy with a stubborn cow that wouldn't go into its stall no matter how hard Lee tried to push and coax. The cow let loose a noxious blast of gas. "I swear to God," said Lee, laughing, "it was on purpose, just to spite me."

Smitty had never seen Lee so animated. But he wanted to make sure the school would be the right fit academically. He asked about classes.

Lee described a feminism class he attended with five kids and a professor. The kids had read four hundred pages of Freud. "They talked about how women envied men because they don't have penises," Lee said, laughing again. "I don't see what that has to do with feminism, but whatever." Still, he liked the rigor of four hundred pages of Freud, and the edgy debate.

Lee especially admired the Deep Springs tradition of self-governance. The twenty-six students helped run the school. They even served as the admissions committee. The second day, Lee was interviewed by eight students and a professor across an imposing table.

Lee admitted to being nervous. Unlike the alum interviews for schools like Princeton, this one mattered and he wanted to make a good impression. They asked detailed questions about his essay questioning religion. They had read it carefully. Then they prodded him for his take on the school's philosophy.

"Do you see a problem with a person in a higher level of society doing menial chores like we're doing?" one student asked.

Another wanted to hear Lee's view on the difference between a passion and a need.

As Lee related all this, Smitty noticed the same upbeat expression he'd had while singing in the holiday choir in December. This wasn't always a lighthearted kid, but he was right now.

"A hypothetical," Smitty said. "If you're accepted to Princeton and Deep Springs, where do you think you would go?"

"Deep Springs," Lee declared without hesitation.

"Really?"

"If I could go right now, I'd just drop the rest of high school."

Smitty asked why.

"My biggest fear is growing up," Lee responded. "My second biggest fear is not being able to grow up."

Smitty wasn't sure what that meant.

"At any other college, I can go live in my own dorm," Lee explained, "have a credit card that's funded by my parents, go party every night, and then, in the godforsaken hours of the morning, study for the test I might have the next day."

Smitty couldn't help but smile. That pretty much captured a lot of kids' college experiences. He wished those who found Lee detached could see this side of him.

The credit-card-and-party life, said Lee, just didn't appeal to him. He preferred the Deep Springs idea of self-sufficiency.

"If you don't milk the cows," he said, "if you don't collect the eggs, you don't eat."

Smitty wondered if Lee was just high off the visit or had truly found the perfect college.

Lee seemed certain. "The things that you would learn at Deep Springs you can't learn at any other college," he said. "It's not only about learning academics. It's about growing up."

Finally, it was time to go. Lee stood, grabbed his backpack, and, in a rush of energy, headed out.

In all his years at Oyster Bay, Smitty felt this might rank as the most unexpected choice. Here was a top student and musician who'd been brought up in a high-achieving culture saying he wanted to go to a little-known college on a working farm.

After decades as a professional college picker, Smitty liked to think he knew how to match a student to a school. Lee Kim was a reminder that he should never make assumptions.

TWENTY-SIX

The Month of Indecision

Chelsea Flynn was torn between a big-city northern campus and a comfortable southern campus. She wanted Mr. Smith's advice. Sometimes she felt that he knew her better than she knew herself.

It was April 1, the Tuesday of the week millions of American high school seniors had been waiting for. The verdicts from almost all colleges were in.

In Chelsea's case, both NYU and the College of Charleston had said yes. So had the University of Vermont, Hobart, Tulane, and Binghamton. They wanted her at Loyola in New Orleans and at New Paltz in the Shawangunks. Skidmore had put Chelsea's name on the wait list. Only Middlebury had said no.

Smitty had driven to school that morning in an upbeat mood, past dogwood trees starting to flower. April was almost always a good time for him. There were a few disappointments, of course, but all his kids had gotten in somewhere, and now, after nine months of trying to impress admissions offices, the Oyster Bay class of '08 had turned into buyers instead of sellers.

It was time for colleges to do the wooing, with calls, alumni barbecues, and campus gatherings.

Smitty had Chelsea go over her choices. Which schools, he asked, was she *least* interested in? He had learned it's a good way to start these discussions—by having kids see where they don't want to go.

Chelsea was a step ahead of him. She was already down to NYU and Charleston.

In Smitty's eyes, it was one of those choices that defines a kid: urban campus versus traditional; private versus public; near versus far. The critical test was whether NYU's prestige was a draw for her. This year it had accepted just 24 percent of applicants, down from 32 percent a year earlier. Chelsea liked to say she didn't care about brand names, but Smitty found that a college with national cachet generally turns kids' heads. There was no question that a typical student from the New York suburbs would take NYU over Charleston.

But Chelsea wasn't ready to decide. In fact, she made it harder on herself. She had asked Skidmore to keep her name in play on the wait list.

Most colleges want nonrefundable deposits by May 1. That would give Chelsea a month, during which she planned to go to both Charleston and NYU for on-campus receptions.

Smitty grinned. "Young lady," he said, "you're going to keep me on my toes for as long as possible, aren't you?"

Chelsea was typical of a trend. In the 1980s and even the 1990s, students applied to five or six colleges. Now that kids applied to so many, it was common to have six or more acceptances.

Riana Tyson had plenty. She had been opening one yes after another: the University of Miami, Northeastern, Pitt, and Spelman, among others. Just one had turned her down: Georgia Institute of Technology.

She, too, went through Smitty's exercise of crossing out the colleges that didn't interest her. It made her realize she wanted to try something far from New York, preferably in a warm climate.

Riana wasn't sure she would have that luxury. Her mom's layoff meant money was now not just one factor but *the* factor. After a year of getting herself into pricey schools, Riana suddenly couldn't afford them, even though most gave her considerable aid. She got grants from $20,000 to $35,000 a year, but if total costs were $50,000, that still left her with $15,000 in annual loans. She was already thinking of grad school, and couldn't picture starting it with more than $60,000 in debt.

She told Smitty she had come to a decision. Did he remember the day he came back from a visit to Manhattan schools and talked up the one with Gothic buildings, student diversity, laundry machines that texted, and, most important, a $4,000 tuition for state residents?

Yes, he did remember.

"You did a good sales job," she said. She planned to attend the City College of New York.

The other Oyster Bay student who'd applied to Georgia Tech was Riana's boyfriend, Andreas Dukas. He had gotten in but thought he would feel more comfortable in New York State. He wanted to be close to Riana, and to his parents.

Plus there was the price difference: His parents owned an ice cream store. They'd saved and were willing to help him with whatever he chose. Still, he couldn't justify spending three times as much to go to some other state's public university when he'd gotten into Binghamton, the flagship of the New York system.

For most applicants to prestigious universities, 2008 was the year of rejection. Harvard admitted just 7.1 percent, compared to 9 percent the year before. Brown said no to 784 valedictorians. In a reflection of the economy, state schools saw a surge in applications. Binghamton admitted less than 40 percent for the first time.

Lee Kim walked into Smitty's office that April 1 morning looking haggard. His family had moved to Queens so that his father could be closer to work. Lee had been busy unpacking. He had some college news. McGill in Canada had admitted him, but he didn't want to go. "It was a safety," he explained.

Smitty didn't say anything. McGill was known as the "Harvard of Canada." Lee saw it as a safety?

Lee had also gotten a yes from NYU, but he didn't want to go. It was much too close to home. He wanted independence.

He'd been surprised by a third acceptance. After he'd been rejected by the economics program he wanted at Oxford, he had been accepted by another university in Oxford, England—thanks to a box he'd unthinkingly checked on the British Common Application. But again, Lee wasn't interested. "A third-rate school," he said with a scowl.

He still had his heart set on Deep Springs, but those letters wouldn't go out for two more weeks.

Smitty asked about Lee's other fifteen-plus schools. What did they decide?

"I don't know."

"Excuse me—you don't *know?*" Smitty wondered if this was some kind of April Fools' joke.

Lee explained that because of his family's move, their Internet connection was down and the post office was holding the mail.

The most selective schools had revealed their decisions the day before. Across the country, seniors had hovered over keyboards, and yet Lee hadn't even looked. Wasn't he curious?

Yes, said Lee, a little. He asked to check on Smitty's computer. Smitty got out of his chair and offered to leave the room if Lee wanted privacy, but the boy shrugged.

Lee wrote out a list of colleges that he hadn't heard from, then went onto the Web.

He went to Yale's site and tapped a few keys. There was a letter saying that, with regret, they had denied his application.

Lee read aloud the phrases Yale offered to ease the disappointment: "'. . . difficult for us to point to obvious weaknesses . . . decisions say far more about the small number of spaces available.'"

Lee didn't react. Smitty couldn't tell if he was upset or indifferent.

Lee wrote the word *No* next to Yale's name.

Smitty stood to the side, silent.

Then the Harvard site: No.

Princeton: No.

Columbia: No.

Lee wrote those answers down, too. Smitty tried to find some reaction on Lee's face. Mostly, the boy looked resigned.

Dartmouth: No.

Duke: No.

Smitty added it up. Lee had just been rejected by six in a row. And then:

Stanford: No.

Vanderbilt: No.

Admittedly, they were among the toughest schools in the country, but eight rejections in a few minutes was a blow to anyone. Although Lee kept up his poker face, Smitty suspected he was crestfallen. Smitty wasn't sure what to say to the boy, though he didn't think Lee wanted to hear a pep talk.

"I'm sorry," he said, and left it at that.

Lee folded up the piece of paper and walked out without a word.

Smitty tried to figure out what had gone wrong. It was a competitive year, and by the standards of Ivy colleges, Lee's 1410 SAT wasn't phenomenal. Smitty also knew that top colleges, without admitting it, held Asian kids to a high standard because so many were overachievers.

Still, Smitty felt there were other reasons for the string of turndowns. Lee sometimes came off as aloof, even arrogant. Lee's heart hadn't been in it, and colleges pick up on that. Smitty didn't think kids should falsely curry favor or overmarket themselves, but, as in much of life, college applicants have to put on their best face, and Lee hadn't.

Except, perhaps, at one college: Deep Springs. There, Lee had done his best. Smitty knew fellow students served as the admissions committee. He hoped, being peers, they were likelier to understand what Lee had to offer.

The wait lists at American colleges had never been longer than in 2008. Smitty couldn't remember a year when so many kids were left in the lurch. Cornell's list had 3,000 kids, almost enough to fill the 3,050 spots in the freshman class. Four Oyster Bay students were among the 3,000. The University of Virginia list had 4,000, including the Oyster Bay boy who had written the "ass" essay.

Not long ago, the wait list had a straightforward message: "We like you and hope a space opens for you." Now, Smitty thought, some wait lists were almost cynical. They were courtesy lists, with no real prospects of acceptance, designed to avoid hurting egos. They were meant to keep alumni parents and others happy, or at least happy enough to donate to the next capital campaign.

Chelsea was wait-listed at Skidmore, and Nathaniel Coleman was wait-listed at four places: Cornell, NYU, Carnegie Mellon, and Washington University in St. Louis.

Layla Eran also was wait-listed at four: Columbia, Brown, GWU, and

Vanderbilt. After applying to twenty-eight programs, Layla had almost too many choices. She'd been accepted by seventeen: Adelphi, American, Barnard, BU, Drew, Drexel, Emory, Fordham, Geneseo, McGill, Muhlenberg, Northeastern, NYU, Siena, Stony Brook, UMass, and the University of Miami.

She'd been turned down by two med programs: Stony Brook's and Siena's.

She asked Smitty what she could expect from her wait lists. She had two Ivy schools leaving her in limbo, Brown and her first choice, Columbia. What were her chances?

The strategy was simple, Smitty said—you write a letter saying you've grown during this year and are more sure than ever of wanting to attend. Remembering her essays, he warned her: "No flowery prose."

And keep it short. "The admissions offices won't admit it," he added, "but they're tired now."

Layla was following admissions gossip on the blogs of Columbia students, and she'd seen comments that the wait list was moving. Smitty warned her there were things beyond her control. If Columbia wanted more kids from Alaska, or an oboe player, that's who they'd take.

A few days later, Smitty was in the school parking lot when Nathaniel Coleman's mother pulled up in her car. Despite the early rejection from Columbia, Nathaniel's college quest had gone well: He'd been accepted at BU, Vermont, Northeastern, Worcester Polytechnic, Rensselaer Polytechnic, and Case Western. He'd been turned down by MIT.

Nathaniel was happy with his six options. He was leaning toward Worcester, where his best friend Evan had already decided to study engineering. They'd visited the campus together, and a student had shown them around a new four-story bioengineering center with a lab featuring something called an atomic-force microscope. Nathaniel could envision himself pulling all-nighters in those labs.

Still, his mom told Smitty that she and Nathaniel hoped to get accepted off Cornell's wait list. She asked if he would edit the letter to Cornell.

Smitty said he'd be happy to. "Just have him bring it to me as soon as he's written it."

Nathaniel's mom corrected him: *She* was writing the letter.

Cornell was crowing about this admissions season. The school's Web site proclaimed it the "Hottest Ivy." It had received a record thirty-three thousand applications, and accepted only 20 percent.

Nathaniel arrived with the letter later that day. "I am writing to you with genuine sincerity," it started. "I long to be a Cornellion. The Cornell Symphony Orchestra calls to me."

Smitty struck out those lines. He kept crossing out: "Enclosed are my recent honors and accomplishments. In addition, I have joined the wind ensemble . . ."

When he'd finished doing his cutting, only three sentences remained. Now it was time to help Nathaniel find his own voice.

Deanna took over. She told Nathaniel to be direct. "You basically need to say, 'I have some great choices, but Cornell is still my top choice.' "

It took him a few minutes to type the message, and then write a second draft. When a third draft was done, Deanna okayed the changes. It was his letter now.

Nathaniel signed it, and off it went.

As soon as friends heard of Chelsea's options, they assumed she would choose NYU over Charleston. Some days, a part of her assumed the same. After all, NYU was NYU. Chelsea talked it out with her art teacher, Ms. Crowley, who had gone to Cornell and knew the advantages of a big-name school. Ms. Crowley said NYU had one of the best photography departments anywhere, and was strong in film and video production, too.

"NYU would give a high-voltage charge to your career," Ms. Crowley said. "You'll get exposure to the most talented people in the field."

Yet Ms. Crowley also saw the advantages of Charleston, saying it would be far more nurturing than NYU.

Ms. Crowley said she sensed that Chelsea's father favored NYU, while Chelsea's mother favored Charleston. As for Ms. Crowley, she wouldn't reveal her favorite; she felt Chelsea needed to decide which campus was more her style.

Chelsea's decision became more complicated when Skidmore took her off the wait list and offered her a spot, giving her three options. She visited Skidmore and found the idyllic college—students tossing Frisbees and lying on greens. She saw campuses through her artist's eye, and she liked the way the light filtered through the trees at Skidmore.

Then she went to NYU's welcome day for admitted students. She met young photographers and writers who reminded her of herself. She heard about unbelievable choices of classes and internships. Although she'd applied to NYU's College of Arts and Sciences, she'd been accepted to something called the General Studies Program, and she went to the admissions office to ask about the difference. No one seemed to have time for her, even though this was a day to welcome new students. Then she went on a tour and they showed something called a "model" dorm instead of a real one. At a speech, NYU's president boasted that this was an urban campus that didn't need a lawn, and that left Chelsea with a pang; she liked to feel grass under her feet. She left with a sense that she might not feel at home at NYU.

Two weeks later, she and her mother flew to Charleston. Chelsea loved the historic feel of both the city and the campus. As she strolled through the art building, a woman asked if she needed help. She turned out to be the assistant director of the department, and they spent the next forty-five minutes chatting.

Back home, everyone wanted to know where Chelsea was leaning; she avoided the question. As always, she struggled with it until the last minute.

At the end of April, on the eve of the deadline for her decision, she sat down to dinner with her parents and two younger siblings. She asked everyone to close their eyes.

A moment later, she said, "Let's have a toast."

Her parents opened their eyes to see maroon mugs in front of them. One said "Charleston Mom," the other said "Charleston Dad."

S mitty had been congratulating Jeff Sanders again and again in recent weeks.

Jeff would stop by the office to say, "Mr. Smith, I got into Seton Hall!" A few days later: "St. John's, Mr. Smith!" Then Towson in Maryland came through. That was one of Jeff's favorites. Jeff had applied to eight schools, and all accepted him. Now he had to decide.

Soon, he headed out to see West Virginia University. Before Jeff left, Smitty guessed that it would be one of Jeff's leading choices. West Virginia was a rah-rah school with a good basketball program. It was also among the public schools that had produced the most Rhodes Scholars.

When he returned from his trip south, Jeff sat with Smitty, earnest and straight-backed. Smitty had noticed that once Jeff's grades improved, so had his posture.

Jeff said he'd made up his mind: West Virginia. He described a great meeting with the basketball coach. He'd brought the coach dossiers of promising future high school recruits; the coach was so impressed, he asked if Jeff would stay at West Virginia after earning his bachelor's degree and be a graduate assistant helping with the sports program.

"You're kidding!" said Smitty, his eyes wide.

Smitty reminded Jeff to keep up his grades. Not long ago, Oyster Bay High had heard from an Ivy League university that had put an entering freshman on probation after receiving an appalling transcript from the final months of twelfth grade. Even as Smitty spoke to Jeff, though, he realized that the warning was unnecessary. Many times he'd worried whether Jeff could stay focused enough to finish high school, and here he was making postgraduate plans.

Smitty had long ago told his kids that ideally, a college should be the start of a life plan. Jeff Sanders had heard him.

TWENTY-SEVEN

"It's About the Kids"

The school band played "Pomp and Circumstance." It was commencement day, the last Sunday of June. The graduation was taking place outdoors. Parents and guests looked on from the lawn below as the Oyster Bay High class of 2008 emerged from the building in caps and gowns onto a stone terrace that served as a stage. They sat in folding chairs, flanked on the left and right by the faculty. The kids fanned themselves with programs in the hot sun.

For Smitty, who wore a black robe, this would be his last graduation. He had become a guidance counselor in 1971, and, after a lifetime of it, was about to retire.

For weeks, his colleagues had tried to get him to agree to a retirement ceremony, but he declined. He felt the end-of-year focus should not be on him. "It's about the kids," he said. Besides, he had never liked a fuss made over him in public. It made him uncomfortable. At a meeting of Long Island guidance counselors a few weeks before, they had ignored his wishes and arranged a send-off from the podium by his friend Mary Beth Carey, who oversaw the Drew University admissions department.

"He swings doors wide open to places the student may have never even thought to peek through," she had said. As she went on, he had shifted in his seat.

And now, as he sat on the terrace, it happened again. The principal stepped to the microphone and said there would actually not be 109 graduates this day, but 110. Mr. Smith had been named an honorary member of the class.

The crowd applauded as he was called forward. The principal spoke of all Smitty had done for Oyster Bay's students for the past nine years. By now, he'd helped more than a thousand find their paths.

"Most important," the principal said, addressing Smitty directly, "you are leaving behind a legacy of truth and fairness." Kathi Reilly, sitting with several other teachers in the front row, joined the audience in a standing ovation.

Smitty was relieved as he sat back down, holding his honorary degree. Soon, it was the turn of each member of the class to go up.

He looked among the faces for his special projects—Riana, Allyson, and Chelsea. Lee was singing in the chorus; Jeff grinned at Smitty. Some in the class had managed to surprise the guidance guru in the last few weeks. Lee had been rejected by Deep Springs, and went to tour NYU with little enthusiasm. Yet he came back excited about the kids he'd met.

Riana's boyfriend, Andreas, sent his deposit to Binghamton, then got news that Georgia Tech's alumni association offered him a scholarship that made the school as affordable as Binghanton. Riana told him he couldn't say no. By summer's end, he would be heading to Atlanta.

Nathaniel had joined the chorus, now that he was trying activities for fun, and not for a college résumé. He'd turned down well-known BU—

his mother's choice—in favor of Worcester Polytechnic, where he felt comfortable. His best friend, Evan, had put down a deposit at Worcester, but decided he couldn't afford it. Evan would be living at home and commuting to Long Island University, which had given him a scholarship.

Now Smitty watched as Layla Eran delivered the valedictorian's address, joking about how she spent so much time at school, she should pay rent. He remembered when he and she would be the last two in the building, and how he would hear her typing on her laptop as he headed home.

Soon after Layla was done, Smitty was asked to rise and come to the podium a second time. It was his role to award the coach's memorial scholarship for a student who had shown remarkable character on and off the field. In the distance, beyond the seated parents, a special few attendees had come to witness this moment. They were volunteers with the fire department, who had parked a hook and ladder truck within view of the ceremony. A white sheet fluttered from the ladder with a message: "Congratulations Jeff Sanders." As Smitty called up Jeff to receive the five-thousand-dollar check, the crew sounded the truck's horn, and it echoed across the campus.

After the last diploma was handed out, grandparents and parents came up to hug the new graduates and pose for pictures. That sunlit setting, with Main Street and the harbor as a backdrop, brought to mind Theodore Roosevelt's observation that Oyster Bay was an ideal place to bring up children. As custodians started to fold up the chairs on the lawn, the kids rushed inside to change from their robes. Smitty went inside, too. One after another, parents and students thanked and embraced him. Gradually they drifted off, and he was among the last in the building.

He went into the guidance suite. A fresh stack of blank pennants waited on Blossom's desk, ready to be filled in with the names and colleges of next year's seniors.

After previous graduations, Smitty had always been struck by the symbolism of staying behind as his kids went forth. Not this year.

Gwyeth Smith Jr. locked his office door for the last time.

And then, much like the Oyster Bay class of 2008, he moved on to the next chapter of his life.

TWENTY-EIGHT

College Student

Jeff Sanders hustled along a sidewalk on the campus of West Virginia University, immersed in a familiar thought: How was he going to tackle everything he needed to do today?

In the next few hours, he had to draft an English essay, finish the reading for a course about post–Civil War history, go to a class, and meet with the basketball coach. The campus was so large that he would have to take the school's shuttle to get everywhere on time. He reminded himself that things would soon get busier. Once basketball season started, he'd be at the gym seven days a week helping as the assistant team manager.

When up against this kind of pressure in high school, he often let his class assignments slide. College was different. He liked the work. The Civil War course helped him understand the South, where he was living, and as part of his effort to work with athletes, he was learning the structure of the human body. Now that he had the option of sleeping late and skipping class, he didn't.

Jeff even liked the required classes. Before the school year started, freshmen at WVU could choose among several intense short courses that allowed them to bond through outdoor experience. Jeff signed up for five days of camping and white-water rafting. Having never been a Boy Scout or wilderness type, he hung back and observed for the first couple of days. Then they needed someone strong to steer a six-person raft down some rapids, and his boat mates turned to him. He made it through, even as a few of the other boats capsized among screams and laughter.

At night, after setting up camp, they had talked about making the transition to college. Counselors warned kids about things like binge drinking, and Jeff, more than some, understood, having seen his share of teen car accidents while volunteering for the Oyster Bay fire department. They discussed time management, too, and college life in general. He formed friendships, and by the time freshman year officially kicked off, Jeff Sanders felt he was a part of West Virginia University.

Soon, he found himself with his first writing assignment—a four-page essay for English 101. Jeff opened his laptop. One of his roommates was talking on his cell, another was playing music, and a friend was surfing TV channels. It reminded him of his own rambunctious home. It didn't take him more than a couple of minutes to find his flow. Just as he'd done for Mr. Smith and Ms. Reilly during senior year, Jeff made an outline in his head and started typing.

Not long after, the professor handed the essays back. Jeff looked at the comments. The professor liked the way Jeff used the active voice and worked in specifics. His grade was an A.

Jeff Sanders had found his fit.

Epilogue

Lee Kim

Looking back, on a December day six months after graduating from high school, Lee was relieved that Deep Springs had turned him down. He wondered whether the student-faculty admissions committee there saw what he should have seen himself: that he wasn't meant to be on an all-boys ranch in the desert. He enrolled in NYU instead. With its urban energy and driven, cerebral students, he became convinced it was just the right college.

Lee also realized something about himself: He had indeed been a bit arrogant. The epiphany came while he was reading about Socrates for an NYU freshman seminar, called "Conversations of the West: Antiquity and Enlightenment."

"When I was in high school, I thought I knew everything," Lee said. "When I came to college, I saw I knew nothing."

Chelsea Flynn

True to her word, Chelsea agonized about her college decision, then never looked back once she made it. She quickly found a community of writers, photographers, and athletes at the College of Charleston. She liked the way the city and the campus were interrelated. "It's not a little bubble," she said as her freshman year ended.

Living in the South, she added, "has exposed me to all kinds of things." The only drawback, Chelsea said, was being far from her family.

Jeff Sanders

Jeff enrolled in West Virginia University and found his calling as a sports management major working with the basketball coach and team as an assistant manager. He maintained a grade point average of 3.72.

Allyson Frankel

Allyson Frankel quickly fell in love with the University of Michigan, particularly its huge size. She discovered a rah-rah university the ideal place for meeting new people from all backgrounds. "This is everything I wanted college to be," Allyson said one day as she was getting ready to pledge a sorority.

Riana Tyson

Despite City College's courtyards and Gothic buildings, Riana encountered more of an urban campus than she expected. After spending her life in the New York area, she wondered if she was ready for a change of scene, and considered transferring. But she was also realizing it would be hard to match City College's four-thousand-dollar annual tuition. Halfway through freshman year, she was still searching for something affordable outside the state. Seeking advice, she called Smitty, who said her 3.925 GPA would help pique the interest of other colleges.

Layla Eran

Layla Eran, at Barnard College, landed at the right place. She was happy. She felt she should have seen it earlier in her application process, before she sent packages to twenty-eight programs. Classes at Barnard and Columbia exposed her to all kinds of career options, and she was no longer certain she wanted to go to med school and become a psychiatrist.

Nathaniel Coleman

From the first days at Worcester Polytechnic, Nathaniel felt at home. He dropped crew because he no longer needed to impress colleges, and joined an intramural fencing team because that's what he wanted to do. For a student who had loved to build Lego structures as a little boy, and even more complex models over the years, engineering school seemed perfect.

Looking back, Nathaniel realized that he'd applied to several colleges mainly because his parents wanted him to. Yet he wasn't upset. "I'm really grateful that they did push me to go to the best school," he said. "I understand they just want to see me do the best I can."

Andreas

Andreas found his first few weeks of engineering courses difficult at Georgia Tech, but slowly settled into a rhythm. He joined the Hellenic Club so he could meet others who spoke Greek, and soon came to see Georgia as the perfect place for him.

Curtis

Curtis, who had won the Horatio Alger Scholarship, left the University of Miami after one semester. Too many Miami students, he said, were just interested in partying. He returned home to go to a community college.

Kasper

Kasper enrolled in NYU and, like Lee Kim, found its intellectual, urban mix a perfect fit. He made friends easily and said he was following his father's advice: "Whatever you do in life, do it well."

Jenna

Jeff's girlfriend, Jenna, liked her courses at Barnard College, and hoped to become an endocrinologist working with diabetic children, yet she was disappointed in Barnard's social life. By the middle of freshman year, she was considering a transfer, but Barnard had covered all her costs, and she knew it would be difficult to duplicate. In retrospect, she thinks she should not have rushed to apply early. She called Smitty, who repeated one of his favorite phrases, "Education is a business decision." By that, he meant not to walk away from a grant worth about $200,000. Smitty told her to give Barnard more time. In high school, she was the bright, driven homecoming queen who dated the quarterback. Smitty suspected she was like many high school stars, feeling lost on a big campus full of other top achievers. Often such kids grow more comfortable, Smitty said.

Dominique

It took several months for Dominique, the actress, to find her place at Emerson College in Boston. "The atmosphere is very competitive and the criticism is very harsh," she said in an e-mail in April of her first year. For a while, she wondered if she'd landed at the wrong place. By the spring, though, she'd appeared in several student productions and she was grateful for all she'd learned about theater.

Colin

In April of his freshman year at Dartmouth, a few days after a close loss in a crew race to Harvard, Colin took stock of his Ivy League experience.

"I'm taking classes with professors who hold us responsible for our own learning, and that's something that most high schools simply cannot do," he wrote in an e-mail. He planned on being a government major and economics minor, focusing on international trade and relations. He was enamored of the classes, social life, and crew. "As I close out the year, I cannot picture myself anywhere else."

Kathi Reilly

Kathi continued on at Oyster Bay, running Essay Writing for College without Smitty. Sometimes, her kids would ask questions she couldn't answer about testing, financial aid, or specific colleges. She kept responding with the same line she used for years: "Let's call down to Mr. Smith." And then she would remember he was no longer there.

Smitty

Gwyeth Smith Jr. had often urged parents to see college as only a beginning. He'd stressed that education doesn't stop the day someone earns a diploma. As a retiree, he followed that advice, finding more time to do reading, particularly on his newfound interest in Abraham Lincoln.

He put out the word that he was opening a private practice to advise college applicants. Within a few months, he had thirty clients, with more prospects calling every week for his $330-per-hour services. Some parents even wanted help for their tenth graders.

He noticed that the parents sometimes needed more counseling than the children. During one introductory meeting, a father started grilling Smitty. "Do you have any guarantees?" the father asked.

Smitty answered with another question: "Do you have guarantees that you'll be on this earth tomorrow?"

He was hired.

Smitty sometimes ponders an irony: In his public school career, he made a name for himself helping working-class and middle-class parents, and yet now he was tending to more affluent families who could afford a private counselor. Still, he was relieved to move beyond the paperwork and endless meetings of a school. To share his good fortune, Smitty took on plenty of pro bono clients: a woman whose husband had left her; a father who had lost his job; a family struggling to pay the mortgage. He wrote opinion pieces calling for more students to take a gap year and do service, and he searched for a foundation that would help him improve college advising for poor and working class students. Mostly, Smitty liked helping kids find their paths. Although it had been time to move on from Oyster Bay High, he remained in the business of guiding and counseling. This, he felt, is what he was meant to do.

Updates will be posted on www.DaveMarcus.com.

When I set out to chronicle the last year on the job of a high school counselor, I decided to blend two very different genres of writing. One is narrative nonfiction. The second is what can best be described as a reader-friendly how-to guide.

The guide part probably is obvious. I wanted to let Gwyeth Smith Jr. impart lessons from nearly four decades of working with college applicants.

Narrative nonfiction, however, requires an explanation. Also called "immersion journalism," it teases out stories from people over a period of time. The writer decides what's important, and tries to bring clarity to the chaos of daily life.

To do this, I spent a year of preparation getting to know Smith and the rhythms of the twelfth grade at Oyster Bay High School. The following year, I watched the class of 2008 go through the application process. I sat with the students in school, ate lunch with teachers in the faculty lounge, attended concerts, and visited several parents in their homes and workplaces. I got insights from faculty members including Dennis O'Hara, Oyster Bay's principal; and Matt Brown, the social worker. I debriefed Gwyeth Smith Jr. and English teacher Kathi Reilly at least three nights a week. I accompanied Smith to a counselors' conference in Austin, and toured a campus with him in Pittsburgh.

I recorded many of the conversations, with permission, so that I could get accurate quotes and learn the cadence of people's voices.

Because I had my own children to care for and a job at a newspaper, I hired two researchers to be my eyes and ears at times. I also tried something I'd never done before: reporting by speakerphone. When I couldn't get to Oyster Bay or when I felt my presence would be a distraction, I listened in on conversations electronically. Each time, Smith and his students allowed me to do this.

The Oyster Bay–East Norwich Central School District was receptive to this project and issued me a photo ID badge. It allowed me to move freely around the school. I'm grateful that the administrators felt confident enough in their staff and students to give me complete access to classes, meetings, and after-school activities. Several faculty members allowed me to read recommendation letters, transcripts, and e-mails, and dozens of current and past Oyster Bay students gave me permission to excerpt their essays.

Oyster Bay High's cooperation is especially remarkable because three years earlier, on my first day as a *Newsday* reporter, I wrote an article critical of the school's use of a group that put on shows about bullying, but then lured students to churches in order to proselytize to them.

These are true stories. I did not change details. I did, however, alter the names of the kids and their parents to protect privacy. This relative anonymity made students and parents comfortable sharing very personal stories with me. (If a pseudonym is the same as someone else's real name, that's a coincidence) Of course, I used the real names of Oyster Bay faculty members and college officials.

When recounting a conversation or event that I didn't watch, I tried to interview all participants to reconstruct it. When I indicate what a person was thinking at a certain time, I'm basing that on his or her recollections.

Although Smith doesn't believe that kids should be summed up by rankings and test results, I did choose to introduce each main character with a few such numbers. Yet the premise of this book is to get beyond scores and stats, to paint human portraits of college applicants.

Upon completing the manuscript, I chose to let Smith, Reilly, and the kids read relevant portions so they could help make it as accurate as possible. I think the result is a truer and more precise narrative.

While working on this project, I volunteered as an alum interviewer for Brown University in order to see the application process from another perspective. I'd recently spent a year as a fellow at Deerfield Academy in Massachusetts, where I taught English and helped seniors with applications. Before that, I'd covered higher education for *U.S. News & World Report*. In short, I'd been pondering the world of college admissions—from both sides—for many years.

My variety of experiences persuaded adults and teens in Oyster Bay to open their lives to me. I appreciate the trust, and I hope this book shows I was worthy of it.

This list includes colleges that many families ignore. These range from colleges for underachievers to those for top students. They include state universities as well as private colleges.

North/Northeast

- Stonehill College, Massachusetts
- Allegheny College, Pennsylvania
- Muhlenberg College, Pennsylvania
- Juniata College, Pennsylvania
- Roger Williams College, Rhode Island
- Monmouth University, New Jersey
- Alfred University, New York
- Hobart & William Smith Colleges, New York
- Marist College, New York

Mid-Atlantic

- Washington College, Maryland
- St. John's College, Maryland
- Goucher College, Maryland
- University of Mary Washington, Virginia
- James Madison University, Virginia

South/Southeast

- College of Charleston, South Carolina
- High Point University, North Carolina
- East Carolina State University, North Carolina
- Furman University, North Carolina
- Elon University, North Carolina
- University of Tampa, Florida

- University of the South, Tennessee
- Rhodes College, Tennessee
- University of North Carolina at Wilmington
- Berea College, Kentucky

West/Southwest

- University of Dallas, Texas
- Colorado College, Colorado
- Pitzer College, California
- University of Redlands, California

Northwest

- Lewis & Clark College, Oregon
- University of Puget Sound, Washington
- University of Seattle, Washington
- Whitman College, Washington

Midwest

- Kalamazoo College, Michigan
- University of Dayton, Ohio
- Miami University, Ohio
- Hiram College, Ohio
- Kenyon College, Ohio
- College of Wooster, Ohio
- DePauw University, Indiana
- Ripon College, Wisconsin

Compiled by Gwyeth Smith with Phil Macaluso, former college adviser, Cold Spring Harbor High School, New York, and Joanne Kesten, college counselor, Friends Seminary, New York City.

High school curriculum

- Take the most challenging classes you can. Before going to college, you should find out how you cope with difficult courses.
- In general, the rigor of the courses is more important than the grades you get. (Ideally, of course, you should have tough courses and excellent grades.)
- Remember that many competitive colleges ignore A grades in electives such as business and art, so you cannot slack off in core courses.
- Four years of math and at least three years of lab science are essential.
- Colleges preparing students to compete in the global economy like to see fluency in at least one foreign language.
- Consider yourself a generalist in ninth and tenth grades, trying all sorts of extracurricular activities. Then, in eleventh and twelfth grades, do your best to find a specialty and pursue a passion in clubs and activities outside school.

Testing strategies

- Take practice ACT and SAT tests – they're available for free at your guidance office or library. Time yourself and see which test reflects your strengths.
- Test prep is a good investment, but you don't need an individual tutor. Group classes are fine. Also consider the online test prep services.
- While the SAT is sometimes seen as a deceptive test, don't be overly concerned about that image. Parts might be difficult, but

there are very few tricky questions—maybe a couple toward the end of the math section. If you think you've got the right answer, go with it.

- During junior year, take the ACT and compare the results with PSAT scores. Keep in mind that while many parents think the SAT is more important, colleges will consider the ACT just as valid.

- Carefully read the testing requirements for colleges you may consider. Some colleges don't require SAT subject tests for those who submit ACT scores.

- On the SAT reading comprehension section, don't be by daunted by dense or boring passages—just try to get the gist of each paragraph, the main idea. Remember; It's an open book test. You should return to the passage when answering questions.

- For the essay section of the SAT, know several historical events, biographies, and works of literature inside out. Examples: World War II, *The Great Gatsby*, Martin Luther King Jr. Most essay topics will allow you to draw on examples from what you've studied. Many students lose points on the essay because of a lack of supporting details, so mastering a few events and novels can help.

- If you choke on tests, consider the more than eight hundred test-optional colleges on fairtest.org.

- In testing, as in the rest of the application process, more is not always better.

Financial aid planning

- Parents should start considering finances early. Use the FAFSA Forecaster (www.fafsa4caster.ed.gov) in your child's junior year to get a sense of what your estimated family contribution will be.

- During eleventh grade, the student and parents should begin to talk about the cost of college, discussing how much debt different members of the family can take on.

- Don't eliminate colleges for high cost alone. Your aid package may surprise you.

- Students need to learn about the elements of financial aid packages, including scholarships and grants (money that is not paid back), loans (which must be paid back), and work-study (money that is earned).

- Parents should emphasize the hazards of racking up credit card bills at college.

- While the matter of where a student attends college is an educational decision, it is also a business decision. Don't drown in debt.

Choosing a college

- Make a list of "must haves" to help refine your list. Example 1: *must have club rugby, Russian major or minor, airport within one-hour drive.* Example 2: *must have four-year housing guarantee, active Jewish community, suburban campus.* Ignore schools that lack the must haves.

- If you have a "dream" school, make a list of ten things you like about it (without using its name or the word "ivy"), then look for campuses with the same attributes

- Avoid the phrase "safety school." Just as you don't want to spend a lifetime with your "safety spouse," you don't want to spend your undergraduate years at a safety school.

- Split possible colleges into reaches, targets, and reliable schools (those likely to admit you).

- By the end of junior year, come up with a list of twenty possible colleges. By the fall of senior year, winnow the list. For most students, there's no reason to apply to more than eight.

Campus visits

- "Visit differences." Tour a city campus and a rural school, a large campus and a small one. These visits can start in tenth grade—so long as they are casual, low-pressure visits.

- Look at the calendar of the college you plan to visit. Some campuses cancel classes during most of December and May for reading period and exam week; some are essentially shut in January during intercession.

- While you may have to visit a campus on a Friday, be aware that at many colleges students generally don't take classes on Fridays.

- Sit in on a class that matches your interest as well as a course on a subject you've never encountered before.

- Remember that you won't get much of the flavor of a campus during a summer visit, but you have a better chance of finding an admissions officer with a few free minutes.

- Ask students—including some in your possible major—about their experiences. Why did they choose this school? What have they disliked and enjoyed about it thus far? Where would they attend college if they weren't here?

- Sign in at the admissions office. Some schools like evidence of your interest.

- Keep in mind that tour guides are promoters, so take everything they say skeptically. Also remember that prospective applicants—and not parents—should ask the bulk of questions during tours.

- Visit the student union—read the message boards, check out students' interactions, and look at the campus newspapers and magazines.

- A student who has learning disabilities or Attention Deficit-Hyperactivity Disorder should talk to the support center or other campus offices that help students with time management and study habits.

- Girls should visit the campus women's center to ask about safety and social life.
- Parents need to trust kids' gut reactions to a campus—but remember that foul weather or a good-looking tour guide can color a visit for a teenager.

Recommendation letters

- Find ways to connect to at least one teacher of a core subject in eleventh grade, and ask for a recommendation.
- Colleges often like a recommendation from the teacher who gave you a "B" and watched you struggle, rather than the teacher who saw you coast to an "A."
- Give teachers at least six weeks' notice if you want a recommendation letter, and write them thank you notes after the letters are sent.
- Fill out a "brag sheet" for your guidance counselor. Your parents should do the same. Despite the name, this isn't about boasting—it's about revealing talents or obstacles that your counselor should know of before writing a letter.

The interview

- This is your chance to be more than a collection of statistics. View the interview as a conversation between two smart, curious people.
- Prepare for the interview. Come up with several thoughtful questions that can't easily be answered by a guidebook or the college's Web site.
- Dress in "business casual." No jeans and T-shirts.
- Arrive early.
- Take the initiative. Introduce yourself and your parents. Mom and Dad should not introduce you!
- If this is an interview with an alum, relax with the knowledge

that a thirty-minute chat rarely makes or breaks a candidate for many colleges.

The essay

- The essay should give readers a glimpse of you that they won't get from your transcript, test scores, and activity sheet.
- Hook the reader with the opening. Don't waste a lot of words setting up the essay—just launch into it.
- Focus on a small topic, or a moment, even if you want to convey a big idea.
- Be counterintuitive. An essay about a defeat or setback can be far more illuminating than one about a victory.
- Discard unneeded adjectives and adverbs—and that means most of them.
- Avoid pretentious SAT words when simpler ones do the job.
- Show, don't tell. Rather than say, "I'm passionate about ice dancing," describe a competition.
- End in a way that leaves the reader hungry for more.
- Read every essay aloud to make sure it sounds right.
- It's fine to get advice, but make sure the writing is yours.

Gap year

- Consider taking a year off, especially if you have doubts about being mature enough to handle the rigor of college or the decision-making skills needed for independent living.
- A gap year has three key elements: holding a job, taking courses at a community college or elsewhere, and doing public service. It is not a vacation.
- A "gapper" must have a mentor who checks in every week. This can be a teacher, counselor, or aunt, but not a parent. The gapper should keep a daily journal.

Preserving family harmony—and sanity

- Parents should spend whole weekends without discussing college apps. If your son or daughter brings up the subject, that's fine, but don't prolong the discussion.

- Set aside forty minutes or so to go to a diner or coffee shop every week to talk about SATs and ACTs, financial issues, and other application business. Designate that place as your "family guidance office."

- Ask relatives to find conversation starters other than, "Where are you applying?" or "Did your friends get in early?"

- Parents, don't compare your son or daughter to an older sibling who has gone through the process, or to a neighbor.

- Students, don't let the college admissions competition ruin friendships.

- Parents, avoid getting fixated on someone's rankings of "best" colleges. Statistics cannot determine whether your child will like a college. It's about the fit, not the brand.

- Remember, where you go to college is much less important than what you do with your time there.

Compiled by Gwyeth Smith Jr. and David L. Marcus with Lisa Sohmer, Julie Gross, Jessica Gross, Phil Macaluso, Joanne Kesten, Frank Polmilla, and William Shain.

FINDING THE RIGHT FIT

Who are you? What kind of college would you like?

1. What are your study habits?
   a. Studious
   b. Don't really enjoying studying and learning
   c. Mixture—study hard, party enthusiastically on weekends

2. What kind of learner are you?
   a. Do you participate in classroom discussion?
   b. Do you reach out to teachers before or after class?

3. Is the physical environment important to you?
   a. Are you looking for a campus-based setting? The energy of a city?
   b. A small campus? A large "rah-rah" university? Or something in between?
   c. Is distance a consideration? Access to home important?

4. Is the makeup of the student body a major consideration?
   a. Conservative vs. liberal (socially as well as politically)
   b. Politically active vs. not involved
   c. What are your feelings regarding diversity:
      i. Racial
      ii. Ethnic
      iii. Gay, lesbian

5. Do you want a big-time athletic program? Or do you have little interest in watching or participating?

6. Fraternities/sororities: Is Greek life a factor?

7. Weather/climate: Would you prefer to see snow or sun in January?

8. Do you feel you lack direction? Are you burned out? Should you consider a gap year to work, study, and do community service under the guidance of a mentor?

We recommend that a student do this self- assessment on his or her own. Separately, each parent should fill it out to describe the son or daughter. Then get together to compare answers. This is intended for eleventh and twelfth graders.

Compiled by Gwyeth Smith Jr. and David L. Marcus. For more information, see www.DaveMarcus.com

ACKNOWLEDGMENTS

This project is the result of a broken promise.

While I wrote a book several years ago, it so disrupted my life that I vowed to put aside my aspirations to be an author again till my children were grown.

One day, though, my *Newsday* colleague Liane Guenther said something intriguing. "You've got to meet this high school counselor," she said. "He's the silver-haired, anything's-possible admissions guru. He gets to know kids better than their own parents know them."

Soon after that, while watching Smitty at work, I realized I *had* to write about him.

Acceptance grew out of "Seven Seniors, Seven Dreams," a series I wrote for *Newsday*. Editors John Mancini, Rosemary McManus, and Cliff Schechtman gave me time, one of the most precious resources in the newspaper business. While overseeing the series, Joe Haberstroh reminded me that the application process is all about dreaming. Sandy Keenan shared her boundless enthusiasm, and Michael Dobie improved my later stories.

Long ago, at the once-great *Miami Herald*, an editor told me that schools are the perfect place to write about race, social mobility, and other pressing issues. Oyster Bay's schools superintendent Phyllis Harrington agreed. Even though she realized that some parts of this book wouldn't be positive, she ensured that every door opened for me. In the guidance office, Danielle Urtheil, Deanna Cali, Blossom Mehler, and the interns, Carolyn Johnsen and Gerard Spennato, patiently let me observe them.

Of course, none of these pages would be possible without the cooperation of the students and faculty at Oyster Bay High. Gwyeth Smith Jr. and Kathi Reilly, especially, let me sit in on their classes, their meetings, their meals. Most important, they allowed me to see them work magic with students making the passage from childhood to adulthood.

Anyone reading between the lines knows I'm skeptical of the system that gives wealthy students the advantage of savvy school counselors as well as private educational consultants. Yet when I needed expert readers I turned to private consultants, including Steve Goodman of Top Colleges, Julie Gross of Collegiate Gateway, and Doretta Katzter Goldberg of College Directions. Phil Macaluso allowed me to shadow his travels with Smitty in Pittsburgh, Austin, and beyond. William Shain, former admissions dean at Vanderbilt University and Bowdoin and Macalester colleges, corrected a string of mistakes.

During this hectic time, a terrific team of assistants had my back. Jaime Frydman, Oyster Bay High class of 2007, served as my first guide at the school. David Krantz, a young journalist, took the best notes I've ever seen. Hana Alberts, also on her way to a journalism career, bonded with the kids and gave me great insights. Marc Beja, an NYU student, sent me statistics, while Eleni Fatsis checked facts and transcribed recordings. Just when I was approaching deadline, the indefatigable Matthew Sawh, fresh out of college, critiqued the manuscript and ferreted out details. My first draft came alive under the tutelage of Tom French, the Smitty of narrative journalism.

Mark Patinkin, a *Providence Journal* columnist, ripped the manuscript apart, then stitched it gracefully together. I've considered Mark a mentor since I profiled him for the Brown University student newspaper, and I'm awed by his talent as a writer. As he did with my first book, Eamon Dolan showed me how to tell the stories and refined them through several drafts. Eamon is the best editor in the business—Maxwell Perkins with a BlackBerry. My agent, Stuart Krichevsky, helped me find the larger meaning in the story of one school counselor. At Stuart's office and at the Penguin Press, I was lucky to work with Kathryn Wick, Laura Stickney, Nicole Hughes, and Randee Marullo.

I treasure the advice from writers, educators, and parents who read early drafts of the manuscript, including Mike Cohen, Lisa Gossels, Matt Reichert, Dan Schuchat, Lori Laubich, Adam Pliskin, Jessica Gross, Elizabeth Edersheim, Karen Dimaggio, Beth Whitehouse, Sarah Dorfman, Sarah Buttenwieser, and Ed Sevilla. Smith College professor Sam Intrator and his Growing Up American class were sharp critics. Pete Kanter once again smoothed out the rough patches in my prose. Smitty's daughter, Nicole Smith, welcomed me at her house in Denton, Texas.

After my years as a foreign correspondent, two organizations helped me make the transition back to the United States. The Nieman Foundation restored my faith in the ability of words to change things. The Woodrow Wilson Foundation sent me to college campuses as a fellow so I could try teaching.

Although I think public schools have resisted true innovation for decades, I salute my favorite teacher, Vic Leviatin, cofounder of WISE, which allows students to break free of the structure of high school and plunge into a project during senior year. I'm a writer because of that experience.

This book came at a difficult time. My father, Lloyd Marcus, who had always been my trusted guidance counselor, was gravely ill. Meanwhile, newspaper journalism, my beloved profession, was imploding. I was lucky that my family shared my conviction that this book would send an important message to teens and parents going through the application process. My mother, Alice Marcus, pitched in with child care. Jim and Ellen Marcus offered encouragement and a quiet place to write. John Marcus gave me tips on writing about firefighting. When I couldn't bear reading another article about admissions, Gary Marcus whisked me to the theater.

Incredibly, during a rare break from this project somewhere around Chapter 2, I fell in love with Justine Lachmann. We were married by Chapter 28. She inspires me with her passion and compassion at home and at work. She has a way of making others laugh, and these days that's a true gift. Our wonderful children didn't see much of me for months, unless you count the occasional scowl reflected in a computer screen. I can never make up the time they—*we*—lost. But I can share a parting note:

Benjie, Tatiana, Alexa, and Dashiell: I trust that someday you will benefit from the lessons I learned from Smitty and the class of '08 at Oyster Bay High.

SOURCES

While researching this book, I drew on all sorts of materials in print and on the Web, including college promotional brochures and sites such as www.College Confidential.com. For data about schools, I often turned to www.CollegeBoard.org as well as the colleges' own sites. For admissions stats, I read college newspapers online and checked the information with college public relations offices. For financial aid information, I turned to the authoritative source, www.finaid.org.

While covering education on and off for more than two decades as a reporter, I've visited dozens of campuses. I learned from conversations with the financial aid expert Mark Kantrowitz, author of *FastWeb College Gold*, and the admissions authority Lloyd Thacker, director of the Education Conservancy. I spoke with MIT dean of admissions Marilee Jones about her notion of "giving childhood back to our children," and I was saddened when she was forced to leave her job after she admitted falsifying her résumé. Her message still needs to be heard.

My writing drew inspiration from *The Gatekeepers*, Jacques Steinberg's inside look at Wesleyan University's admissions office. Kristen Laine's *American Band* offered insights into teens and religion. After my friend Barbara Kimmel suggested the title for this book, I learned about the other *Acceptance*, Susan Coll's entertaining novel about admissions.

While I worry about the idea that kids should be groomed for college admissions, I did find worthwhile pointers in *What Colleges Don't Tell You* by Elizabeth Wissner-Gross.

I mention other worthwhile reading at www.DaveMarcus.com.